BILLION DOLLAR MINDSETS

How Smart Relationships Win Government Contracts

Dr. Tom Barrett

Business/Life Management, Inc., VA

BILLION DOLLAR MINDSETS

How Smart Relationships Win Government Contracts

How to order:

To enhance your team's BILLION DOLLAR MINDSETS, copies are available at CommunicationGuys.com/BillionDollarMindsets

Acknowledgements

To Our Warfighters

These courageous men and woman sacrifice every day to keep our freedom. Each day should be Veterans Day and a day to celebrate their commitment. These heroes protect the most important people in my life: My wife, daughters, sons-in-law, and delightful tribe of grandchildren.

To Our Government Contractors

I am regularly amazed at the dedication and passion of government contractors. For years it has been my privilege to get in the trenches with them and see first-hand their genius being used to solve and manage some of the most daunting challenges of our modern world. They too, are unsung heroes. It is my honor to serve them.

To My Good Buds and Life Friends

Success is never a solo event. I've been honored to forge this research and market test this content for years with many people. But two dear friends who are also subject matter experts must be thanked in particular: Ron Ralston and Dave Potts. Without them, this book would never have become a reality. Nor would my life be as satisfying.

To Linda

A sign hanging in our theatre room reads, *My Next Husband Will Be Normal.* There is nothing normal about living with a shrink who spends large amounts of time researching, writing, speaking and traveling. My life, like this book, is far better because of you.

Table of Contents

Introduction: Why this book is different

The Pentagon. Drive down the George Washington Parkway in Northern Virginia and you can't miss it. There it sits, a construction marvel housing 25,000 workers on a daily basis. Impressive and imposing. Intimidating and important. At first glance, it looks inaccessible and impossible to understand. How do you get onto the grounds of the Pentagon? How do you get access into the building? Once inside, what can you do and what must you *not* do? How do you learn to navigate your way around one of the largest office buildings in the world? How do you make sense of its multiple wings, rings, colors, and corridors? And how do you develop an understanding of the people who work there and the programs they manage? It's a daunting undertaking... until you crack the code. To do so, you'll need to think outside the 5-sided box.

Like learning to successfully navigate the Pentagon, this book enables you to crack the code on understanding the largest customer in the world. That customer is not Google or Apple. Costco or Walmart. It's the United States Government and the Department of Defense (DoD) with annual procurements totaling over a trillion dollars.

When doing business with the DoD or any other U.S. Government agency, it is vital to understand that there are laws to learn, cultures to comprehend, and rules to respect. It's a world of incredibly smart and passionate people. It's a world of high tech, high stakes, high speed, and high significance. At times, it's a world of high stress. And at *all* times, it's a world where relationships matter.

After working for over two decades with individuals in this world of procurements, I am constantly reminded that smart customer relationships matter enormously. There is an intangible and unwritten value placed on customer relationships. Source selection can be perceived as an analytical mathematical process where a spreadsheet yields the winner. In practice, smart customer relationships significantly influence evaluation scoring and awards.

The purpose of this book is to:

- Help you understand the extraordinary power of smart customer relationships in this relationship-driven market.

- Explain why you are often only one relationship away from a win or a loss.

- Demonstrate that the greater your skill in building smart relationships *with* the customer, the greater your probability of winning business *from* the customer.

- Teach you the ten power mindsets that create customer preference for your organization.

Within this unique market, I have seen programs, small and large, awarded to contractors who did not have the best price or the most technically superior product. But they did have the best relationship with the customer; one where trust was deep and the customer valued working with the contractor, even when there were programmatic challenges. This book provides you a roadmap to building trust and preference before the Request for Proposal (RFP.)

Style and Assumptions

The foundation of this book is built on researching a compendium of over 90 superb books on relationships, winning and working with the government. I have added my own original research and insights from 20-plus years of hard-fought-for experience.

I suggest that you first read the book from cover to cover. After that, use the book as a reference guide before going into customer engagements. The book is intentionally full of checklists and bullet points for your easy reference and use.

Before jumping into the first chapter, allow me to explain the style of writing I have chosen for this book and some of the assumptions I am making.

According to Einstein, the sign of genius is the ability to say profound things in simple ways. In this book, you will learn insights and mindsets that are career and life changing. But rather than trying to impress you with the technical, insider language many of us use each day, I have selected a writing style that is easy for you as a reader. My hope is that you can read this book on a flight from Denver to D.C. and then immediately apply the skills you learned upon your arrival.

Of course, executives, program managers, engineers and business development people need the skillsets I will examine in the pages ahead. But the reality is that these skills are needed by every individual who has a touch point with the customer.

I will emphasize the importance of smart customer relationships before the government's release of the RFP. And I will show how customer relationships enhance your likelihood of winning awards. However, the primary focus of this book is not to teach how to write winning proposals and excel at orals. It is to emphasize that every customer encounter matters throughout the entire lifecycle of a program – even after the award has been won.

The U.S. Government is made up of more Federal, State and Local agencies, departments, and organizations than it can account for, but for linguistic ease, I speak of the U.S. Government as a single customer and in generic terms. *Federal, Government, Govies* are all terms referring to the customer. Your job is to take the skills and insights in this book and apply them to your specific section of that world.

Like fashion, government contracting relationships are cyclical. But I have chosen to focus on the time-tested jewels and foundational truths of smart relationships. I will also discuss today's dramatic changes and suggest approaches to navigate tomorrow's minefields.

All of the stories you read in this book are true, but I have intentionally changed the names of individuals, randomly changed their gender, and avoided the use of the corporation or program with which they were affiliated. My purpose is to give you real-life wisdom while embarrassing no one.

By the way, most defense firm executives (and most engineers) have an allergic reaction to the word "sales," but I mean it in the new way of being trusted and providing insight, not selling used cars in a plaid suit. So please don't be offended by the "S" word in some quotations.

Finally, in my daily life I have the privilege of chairing meetings and teaching some of the most fascinating and gifted people in the world. At every one of these events, I have two goals. My first goal is for those attending to be grateful that they walked into the meeting. My second goal is for them to be wiser when they walk out of the meeting. I have that same goal for you: May you be grateful that you picked this book up and may you be wiser when you put it down.

Let's get started.

– Dr. Tom Barrett

Part One: Growing your Relationships

Chapter 1
The "X" Factor of
Winning Business

This is a relationship-driven market–make no mistake about it.[1]

Let's begin with a fundamental premise of this book:

The E of L = R

This is a mathematical way of saying that *The Essence of Life Equals Relationships.*

Much of life, including business life, is about relationship management. Organizations that take this natural part of human existence seriously have an uncanny way of having serious success. They know that extraordinary customer relationships are the X Factor differentiating them from the competition when all other factors are equal.

In the current environment, the goal of government procurement is to level the playing field for all bidders and make price a deciding factor. Against this backdrop, it is easy for bidders, especially those unfamiliar with the world of complex sales, to conclude that the X Factor of customer relationships has no bearing on who wins awards from the government. Ostensibly, the only thing that matters is that the proposals submitted to the government are compliant, lowest cost, least risk, and best value. Those deemed most successful in these areas are the certain winners.

It can appear that quantifiable data points have removed human emotion from the award process. In theory, this is true. In real life, not so much. Just ask the incumbent who lost a $450 million re-compete bid. After much wailing and gnashing of teeth, the truth emerged. They lost for only one reason: the customer could no longer stand to work with the provider's program manager. The essence of life is relationships... it can be an expensive lesson to learn. Or, it can be a profitable skill to master.

Author Seth Godin has noted that vanilla is the most popular ice cream flavor, with chocolate being the second. But vanilla sells four times as much. Similarly, those with Billion Dollar Mindsets can win four times as much as an average relationship builder. Like scoring on the Richter scale, the power of skillful customer relationships is logarithmic.

Regarding this premise, consider the quotes and comments below:

- "To succeed in complex sales, the most successful salespeople [bidders] are interacting with their customers by building relationships based on professionalism, trust, and cooperation."[2]

- "Customer relationships are the invisible bubble within which analytical decisions are made."[3]

- "We see our customers as invited guests to a party, and we are the hosts. It's our job every day to make every important aspect of the customer experience a little bit better."[4]

- "Performance is the foundation. Customer relationships are the competitive edge."[5]

Why are customer relationships the X Factor of winning? It's not because awards are given to the government's "buddies." Nor is it because awards are given to those who know how to schmooze with the customer, have the best personality, or the most charm. These have nothing to do with winning. The X Factor of smart customer relationships has a rational explanation. Notice the logic flow of the six points below:

Those who learn the skill of developing a smart relationship with the customer are most likely to have greater ease of access to the customer.

Ease of access to the customer enables you to have more valuable time with the customer.

More time with your customer enables you to have greater understanding of your customer.

More understanding of your customer gives you legal intelligence into the customer's needs, pressures, pain points, and priorities.

Deeper intelligence about your customer enables you to more effectively bring specific value and iterate problem-solving solutions to your customer.

Your intelligence, specific value, and problem-solving solutions can then be represented in a "custom fit" proposal to the customer that clearly differentiates you from the competition.

What's a Mindset?

A mindset is a set of beliefs or way of thinking that determines one's behavior, outlook, and mental attitude. The 10-point BILLION DOLLAR MINDSETS Relationships Compass is an approach to implement the X Factor. The northern point is *Trust*, and its foundation to the south rests on *Listening*. To the west is *Networking* that sets the tone for seeing from your customer's perspective. The east highlights *Awareness*. Throughout this book, we will examine the MINDSETS on the points of the compass.

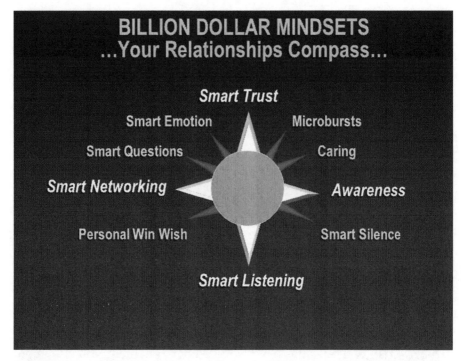

BILLION DOLLAR MINDSETS
...Your Relationships Compass...

Smart Trust

Smart Emotion

Microbursts

Smart Questions

Caring

Smart Networking

Awareness

Personal Win Wish

Smart Silence

Smart Listening

Proposals and awards... where customer relationships are celebrated

In the world of sports, there are culminating moments when we identify the winners of events such as the World Cup, World Series, or the Super Bowl. In the world of procurements, we recognize the winner at the award of "the winning bid." This is when the ROI (Return on Investment) of customer relationships pays dividends. It's the moment when your demonstrated understanding of your customer, fused with your passion and capability to solve their problems, is recognized.

If you have built strong relationships, customer advocacy, gathered critical intelligence and truly understand the multiple stakeholders, you can write a personalized proposal rather than one full of boilerplate text.

Your proposal should FIT like a glove. To make sure it FITs, take the Final Intimacy Test below. When the customers/evaluators read your proposal, here is what they should see and feel:

✓ It should be like a mirror reflecting their visions, hopes, and dreams.

✓ They should experience the wow moment and see your proposal as tailored to their mission needs, like a well-tailored suit.

✓ They should feel comfortable that their fears and biases are addressed.

✓ They should not experience any surprises.

✓ They should feel your shared insights.

✓ They should see solutions to their Real Felt Pain. (RFP #2)

By the way, there are actually *four* RFPs that are part of a Billion Dollar Mindset. Each of them is important to understand. Here's a brief introduction to them.

- RFP #1 is the Request for Proposal released by the government.

- RFP #2 is the customer's Real Felt Pain. (This is what you learn about them.)

- RFP #3 is Really Fabulous People. (This is what they learn about you and your team.)

- RFP #4 is Really Fabulous Presentation. (This is a presentation that, in addition to being fully compliant, is clear, cogent, and connects with the customer at a visceral level.)

Regarding RFP #2, the customer's Real Felt Pain (or real need) is often not stated clearly in RFP #1. Why? Because no one likes to flag shortfalls or gaps. Wouldn't it be great if you could X-ray your customers to find their pain? Short of that, you need to maintain a laser focus on understanding your customer and then reflect that understanding in your proposals and presentations.

Reminders for Maintaining a Customer Focused Mindset

"One way to overcome our natural self-centeredness is to try to see things from other people's perspectives. Talking to a group of salespeople, Art Mortell shared this experience: 'whenever I'm losing at chess, I consistently get up and stand behind my opponent and see the board from his side. Then I start to discover the stupid moves I've made because I can see it from his viewpoint. The challenge is to see the world from the prospect's viewpoint.'"[6]

Think of the words you would like to hear from a customer:

- He's not really a BD (Business Development)/Sales guy; he's a problem solver.

- He never has a hammer looking for a nail.

- I can call her cell any time for insight and trusted advice.

- He understands me and my problems/challenges.

- He gives me what I need, not just what I asked for.

Keep the end in mind:

"The best proposals reflect the language, style and needs of the customer, i.e. they are buyer-centric, not bidder-centric. This is based on a core tenet of rapport-building and empathy: that people tend to most closely identify with and be influenced by people who show they understand them and who they think are most like them."[7]

It is also helpful to watch out for some of the common dysfunctional behaviors of both bidders and customers.

Dysfunctional Behaviors of Bidders:

- We don't talk to the right people

- We try to fit their needs into our solution

- We don't understand their mission

Dysfunctional Behaviors of Customers:

- They don't know what they need.

- They can't articulate what they need.

- They don't agree on what they need.

- They won't give us good information.

- They don't let us talk to the right people.

- They are unrealistic about the time, money and people needed.

- Politics and personal issues count more than business sense.

- They procrastinate.

- They won't make decisions.[8]

You have undoubtedly heard about the number of awards given to children in youth sports. It's hard not to chuckle at the creative efforts made to ensure every child feels like a winner and gets a trophy. In the world of government procurements, there is no such effort, but they do give out a stunning number of awards. While speaking at the 20th Annual Conference of the Association for Proposal Management Professionals, Bob Kempinski noted: *"...with the Federal Government alone approving a bid every 20 seconds of every business day, the number of bids is staggering."* If you want to win some of these, consider my counsel to Rich.

Rich is a small business owner who wanted to win one of these bids. The more he learned about the size of the U.S. Government as a customer, the more he wanted to decipher how to get access into the world of government contracting. Over breakfast, he mentioned what it would mean to his firm, "If we could just get a piece of that pie. Just a small fraction of one percent of the procurement world would transform our company!" As diplomatically as possible, I suggested to Rich that he stop salivating. Then I mentioned that he needed to stop seeking to get a piece of that pie. Instead, he needed to focus on learning how to understand, serve, and bring value to the people represented by that pie. The USG "pie" is not an institution – it's individuals. It's not only about programs; it's about people.

The more skilled you are at establishing a valued relationship *with* them, the easier it becomes to win business *from* them. Let's look at how you can build business-winning relationships that differentiate you from your competitors.

---

[1] Amtower, *Selling to the Government*, 2011, Page 91

[2] Jeff Thull, *Mastering the Complex Sale*, 2003

[3] Burlie Brunson, Ph.D. Scientist in Fortune 100 Company

[4] Jeff Bezos

5 Corporate VP, Fortune 100 company

[6] Maxwell and Dornan, *How to Influence People*, 2013, Page 83

[7] Keyser, 2014

[8] Khalsa and Illig, *Let's Get Real Or Let's Not Play*, 2008, Page 9

Chapter 2
Mission Set, Mindset, and Skillset

Customer Relationships are the Unseen Discriminator of Success.

Paying attention to customer relationships can seem like an irrelevant and inconsequential detail. But just as with fighter pilots, paying attention to "little things" can be the difference between your success and failure.

As a concept, most of us willingly embrace the idea of paying attention to customer relationships. It's a notion that's difficult to argue against. The challenge is moving from acknowledging the notion to acting on it. To move from knowing to doing… from rhetoric to results.

As part of her executive physical, Rachel had to make a trip to her local blood lab for routine testing. She arrived just after eight in the morning and walked into an already crowded waiting room. She knew the drill, so she walked up to the glass partition where the receptionist was sitting. The receptionist was clearly indifferent to her arrival, but she did tell Rachel to sign in, sit down, and wait for her name to be called. Rachel obliged. After 20 minutes, she went up to the window and said, "I'm not trying to hurry you, but can you please tell me how much longer I might have to wait for my blood test?"

With a face that registered zero concern and a voice that confirmed it, the receptionist barely looked up and said, "I have no idea," and then turned away.

As Rachel was returning to her seat, she noticed a proudly posted sign on the left side of the receptionist's window. In large letters, it proclaimed this national lab's promise of customer satisfaction. Below the promise were five principles of Six Sigma. Clearly, something got lost in translation between posting the values of this corporation and the practice of those values by its employees.

This "lost in translation" of customer values is common for both large and small organizations in the government space. Here is an example of one company, and it's actually a representation of many others.

It seemed like a good idea at the time. As the new leader of a Fortune 100 company, the CEO decided to go on an around-the-world listening tour. He wanted to meet personally with the corporation's key customers. Of course, he wanted them to get to know him. More importantly, he wanted to get to know them while hearing firsthand what his most vital customers thought of the enterprise he now led. So off he went to sit face to face with customer counterparts, each representing billions of dollars in major portfolio programs.

He heard great things about the corporation's programs that literally shaped the future of the world. The customers were delighted with technology developments, program deliverables, and software solutions. However, there were too many moments when he had the "I'm sorry I asked" syndrome. Particularly when he asked one specific question: "What's it like to work with us?" His customers were not shy about telling him precisely what it was like to work with his company. The common refrains that emerged were:

1. You don't listen.

2. Stop trying to sell us products that you currently have. Instead, help us solve our problems and give us solutions that we *need.*

3. You are arrogant.

Why does this world-class organization have systemic challenges with customer relationships? Embracing smart customer relations is one of its core values. This value is clearly reflected in the mission statement written on the website and regularly embedded in corporate presentations to customers. And without question, each of the corporate officers understood Sam Walton's conviction that:

"There is only one boss, the customer. And he can fire everybody in the company from the chairman on down, simply by spending his money somewhere else."

So what explains this disconnect between what is purported by the corporation and what is experienced by its customers? The answer is deceptively simple: *They do not know how to shift Smart Customer Relations from a corporate value embraced at headquarters to a behavior that is automatically exhibited in the field by every employee interfacing with customers.*

The challenge of this corporation is not unique. Many organizations miss the distinction between corporate values and corporate culture. To explain the difference, it helps to be clear on what I mean by corporate culture. Let's define it.

Corporate Culture is the beliefs *and the **behaviors*** that are embraced *and **exhibited*** by an organization.

Before zooming ahead with your reading, stop and look at the definition again. Note the words that are in boldface and italics. Corporate culture is *not* a list of beliefs that are identified by corporate leaders who, in turn, make certain that these beliefs are posted on the corporate website and mentioned at the onboarding of new employees by human resource personnel.

Rather, corporate culture is evidenced by corporate beliefs that translate into *behavior* that is *exhibited* at all levels of the organization, starting at the top. These beliefs and behaviors are relentlessly posted, talked about, practiced, looked for, modeled and rewarded.

How do you build an organization with a culture of team members committed to building customer relationships that are so strong that they differentiate you from your competitors? It begins by understanding the linkage of the three components of smart customer relationships. They are represented on the following page.

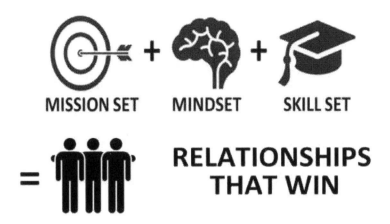

Mission Set

Mission set is identifying who you are as an organization and what you stand for. It is determined at the corporate level and represents the values and visions that drive the behaviors expected of every employee. Regarding customer relationships, it is the identification of the integrity, character, and commitment your customers can expect to see on a regular basis throughout your organization.

Mindset

As difficult as it is for some organizations to specifically articulate the foundational values that drive their organization, it's even harder for them to get employees in the field to embrace and exhibit these values. How do they ensure that key behaviors of smart customer relationships are becoming part of the warp and woof of daily conduct by every teammate? For example, how do they ensure that two years of skillful business development with a potential customer is not put at risk because of an arrogant executive, a clueless engineer, or a contracts person who believes that only facts matter? At the core, the challenge is getting every person in your organization to embrace a mindset of practicing smart customer relationship skills on a daily basis.

Curiously, most employees don't avoid practicing smart customer relationships because they are against the concept. They don't practice smart customer relationships because:

- They don't know *how* to practice becoming more effective at customer relationships.

- They *forget* to practice smart customer relationships.

The second reason is the one I find most fascinating. The concept of practicing smart customer relationships is simply not part of their mindset. It is literally out of sight and out of mind. In the high speed of daily living customer relationships may be a lovely idea, but it's not one they have time to think about, let alone practice.

Harvard Professor, Ranjay Gulati brilliantly stresses the need for corporations to move customer centricity from a shopworn mantra into their way of life.[1] To do this, we need a 24/7 mindset of paying careful attention to those around us. We need to remember, "Customer-centricity is a mind-set you can't afford not to have."[2]

When I speak on this subject, it quickly becomes evident that most organizations have no system in place to help their employees maintain a daily mindset of practicing smart customer relationships. Customer focus is more of an incidental suggestion rather than an absolute priority to be practiced by every person in the organization on a daily basis.

When organizations have only intermittent reminders of the importance of customer relationships, I suggest that they look at Ritz Carlton as a prototype. The organization masterfully understands the interplay of Mission Set, Mindset, and Skillset. It's no accident that Ritz Carlton is viewed as the gold standard of smart customer relationships. Every day, at every Ritz Carlton facility in the world, each team begins by making sure they have a mindset of intentionally paying attention to customer relationships. Every team recites out loud, "We are ladies and gentlemen – serving ladies and gentlemen." And then they examine what this means by reviewing one of their core values. This is a brilliant way to make sure that every employee has the proper mindset with which to greet every customer.

On a lighter note, you might also recall the movie *Tommy Boy*, with Chris Farley. There is a great scene when Tommy Boy is driving in the car with his reluctant mentor – played by David Spade. David asks him to recall the key things to remember while meeting with customers. Tommy thinks as hard as he can, but his mind just draws a blank. After David Spade tells him the answer to his question, Tommy Boy bangs his hand on the dashboard and exclaims, "I knew that! Why can't I remember it?" Maintaining a Mindset of customer-centric focus is easy to forget, but it is vital to remember. Because only after we have the proper mindset can we begin to excel at the Skillset of smart customer relationships.

Skillset

Embracing the Mission Set of your organization is the starting point. Maintaining the Mindset of customer relationships is the challenge. Developing the Skillset of smart customer relationships is the magic.

The rest of this book will explain these skillsets, but let's begin with some baseline insights to consider and keep top of mind.

Government customers have three basic rules of courtesy and respect:

1. Don't waste my time.

2. Don't go around me.

3. Don't surprise me. (Provide me a heads-up on problems or key issues. This means, when lightning bolts come down, coordinate with your customer to help them avoid getting struck.)

Government customers view the first rule as part of their Bill of Rights, so beware not to violate it. Customers want you to:

*   Stop briefing when they get your point.

*   Stop talking when they are not interested in a topic.

*   Stop making their jobs harder.

Be careful not to give them "action items" and more things to do. Shorten the meeting or finish early to give them back some time. (No one gets upset when you give them the gift of time.)

Beware of burning time. When you get asked a simple question that calls for a simple "yes" or "no" answer, just ANSWER it. Avoid long-winded answers and dissertations. If more information is needed, the customer will either look inquisitive or ask for more information.

Along with respecting your customer's time, you might want to consider my version of the *Customer Bill of Rights.*

Customer Bill of Rights

1. *I have the right not to have my time wasted.*

2. *I have the right to reject meetings with any contractor who doesn't provide me knowledge, insight, help and value.*

3. *I have the right not to be bored or subjected to self-serving charts of contractor bravado.*

4. *I have the right to ask questions and get straight answers.*

5. *I have the right to fewer PowerPoint charts and more discussion.*

6. *I have the right to my free speech and to interrupt with questions and take the floor.*

7. *I have the right to trustworthy contractors that are open, transparent and don't surprise me.*

8. *I have the right not to be put at risk or subjected to program failure.*

9. *I have the right to bear arms against being sold to against my will.*

10. *I have the right to like and trust whoever I like and trust.*

Remember, "You are more successful when you concentrate on the success of others rather than on your own."[3]

Make it your Mission to develop a Mindset and learn the Skillsets of smart customer focus. The results are magical.

Mindset Tips:

✓ Don't waste my time.

✓ Don't go around me.

✓ Don't surprise me

1 Gulati, *Reorganize for Resilience*, 2009, Page 9
[2] Miller, Heiman and Tuleja, *The New Successful Large Account Management*, 2005, Page 237
[3] Khalsa and Illig, *Let's Get Real Or Let's Not Play*, 2008, Page 11

Chapter 3
Push the
Relationship

We always get the bidder we want, even after protests. [1]

Peter Drucker, the great management guru, said that there is only one valid definition of business: To create a customer. He also reminded us that in business *the customer is the only profit center.*

If your organization is going to create customers that become profit centers, it is vital for every person in the organization to understand that customer relationships are a key component of this achievement. Every employee needs to be intentional about practicing smart customer relationships at every opportunity. To do this successfully, they need to grasp three things:

1. Why it matters to push customer relationships.

2. What it means to push the relationship with customers.

3. How to qualitatively measure their customer relationships.

Push the Relationship: Why It Matters

The comedian Chris Rock quips: "When you meet somebody for the first time, you're not meeting them, you're meeting their representative." Only when you move past interacting with your customer's representative do you get increased access into who your customer really is and the truth about what he or she wants, needs and values.

But it's fair to ask, if cost is king/queen, does it even matter to move beyond getting to know your customer's representative? In lean budget times, it can seem that everything is being commoditized and that lowest cost is the singular procurement variable. It becomes easy to believe that LPTA (Lowest Price, Technically Acceptable) is the law of the land. (In fact, the pendulum had swung too far towards LPTA until Frank Kendall, Under Secretary of Defense for Acquisition, pulled it back. His Better Buying Power (BBP) initiative stemmed the tide, reverting to best value tradeoffs and monetizing value.)

Of course, for simple commodities like grass cutting and toilet paper, it's still the case that cost is the primary driver. But that isn't the case for complex products and systems. In these arenas, evaluators regularly select the bidder they want, even if the bidder is not the lowest price. (And they regularly get who they want even after protests.)

It's important to understand that bidder relationships can be weighted more heavily than price. Evaluators have ample relationship-based "subjective" factors that legitimately justify their award decision.

Evaluators can't be 100% objective. They are people, not robots, who often have a predisposed bias towards who they want to select. Plus, their evaluation duty requires them to be sequestered for long days under high stress for relatively low compensation, all while still being expected to perform their day job. Not fun. Anyone who makes the experience less painful while facilitating their ability to make a smart and safe decision is highly valued by them.

Against this backdrop, bidders who are known and trusted increase the evaluators' selection confidence. To be that bidder, it's important to understand what it means to "push the relationship" with a customer.

Push the Relationship: What It Means

Having taught the skill of *Push the Relationship* to thousands of individuals in Tier 1 companies as well as small and mid-size corporations, I understand that the words and the concept it represents might be new to you. But while new, its logic and simplicity make it easy to grasp. When individuals or teams take it seriously, it's a positively disruptive skill that sharpens focus, deepens relationships, and wins business. (And for some, it's an eye-opener that explains why they lost business in the past that they should have won.)

To understand the concept, take a moment and observe the graphic below.

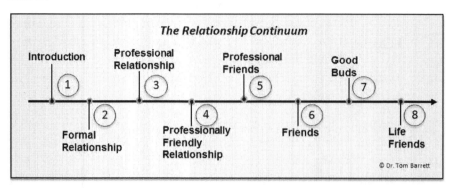

The continuum depicts the eight stages of customer relationship development. These stages are progressive and cumulative. All relationships begin on the left in stage one with the "Introduction." Then, moving right, there is a series of additional relationship stages that can be entered into. As you progress across the continuum, your relationship with the customer deepens. Additionally, each step to the right increases your ability to understand, serve, and bring value to the customer.

The full spectrum of the relationship ends on the far right in stage eight with "Life Friends." While stage eight is real, it's important to understand that becoming life friends with your customer is the rare exception and not the intended norm. It isn't necessary for you to become life friends with your customer, nor is it realistic. You don't have the time or energy to do this, and your customers don't expect it. In fact, many would vigorously resist it. As Peter Garber writes:

"You don't have to become friends with your customers, but treating them more like one can have many positive results for both of you. You will find that treating a customer as you would a friend can result in building a stronger relationship."[2]

The goal of pushing your customer relationship to the right is *not* to get into stages seven or eight. Rather, *the goal is to get you unstuck from stages one and two on the left side of the continuum.* Like a timid swimmer clinging to the edge of a swimming pool, I am stunned at how often I see individuals and teams that have been working with their customer for months or years without ever moving beyond stage one and two. At every customer encounter, they are stuck in an endless loop of being reintroduced, re-establishing rapport, and guardedly interacting with their customer. In these stages, there is little conversational freedom, laughter, or spontaneous human connection and sharing. These encounters have all the thrill of sharing a holiday meal with a distant relative that you barely know and marginally like.

The sweet spot of the continuum is the middle stages. When your relationship with your customer grows to a place where you are professionally friendly, and maybe professional friends who then become friends, you now have a relationship with your customer that is beginning to be a differentiator for you versus your competitors. In these stages, an inherent level of familiarity and trust has developed. And the more these develop, the more invested your customer becomes in being loyal to you and being your advocate at the time of source selection decision. In source selection meetings, they are the ones who pound the table on your behalf, saying, "There is no way I want to go forward on this program without Karen as our lead PM!"

Of course, no customer is going to pound the table as your advocate just because you have a good relationship with them. Developing a stage four, five, or six relationship with your customer is not a "get-out-of-jail-free card." You aren't exempt from providing extraordinary products and program execution. Nor are you exempt from reasonable pricing. These are the non-negotiables.

However, the magic of smart customer relationships in the middle stages is this: *You win the ties.* To make sense of this, let's look at baseball. In baseball, whenever there is a close play between a runner and the fielder, where does the tie go? You probably know the answer: *the tie goes to the runner.* Similarly, when dealing with the government, whenever there is a close call between two bidders who both have equally great products, prices, and solutions, where does the tie go? *The tie goes to the one who has the best relationship with the customer.* Period. All things being equal, your relationship with the customer is your slight edge, the tipping point that bends customer decisions in your favor instead of your competition's favor. To win the ties, *which are very common*, it helps to avoid drinking the Contractor Kool-Aid.

Don't Drink the Kool-Aid!

When working with Tier 1 companies, do you want to know what scares me most? It's those teams who drink their own Kool-Aid. These teams accept the fact that the tie goes to the one who has the best relationship with the customer. However, they cannot accept that there might actually be a tie between their product/solution versus a competitor's. In their minds, they have vast technical superiority, and they are confident that the delta between what they provide versus that of any other provider is so large that they are assured the win. For them, there is no need to pay serious attention to developing, or maintaining, a smart relationship with their customer. They are too valuable and too good to be troubled by such pedestrian concerns.

In a similar fashion, some teams drink the Contractor Kool-Aid of false confidence based on a long history with the customer. In their thinking, they are so embedded with the customer that they are untouchable in a re-compete.

These teams begin to take their customer for granted and become so overly comfortable that they risk complacency (also known as *incumbentitis*). When this false confidence takes root, they lose their edge and stop listening carefully to the customer's concerns and priorities. In their excessive confidence they forget that "big egos have little ears."

A good friend of mine, who is also a brilliant engineer, compares this complacency to first-date behaviors versus a 30-year marriage. On the first date, most guys hold in their gut and have perfect manners, but that tends to fade after decades of marriage. Teams that have been with a customer for years cannot afford to get lazy and miss the customer's suggestions, hints, and signals. They need to remember to treat their customer as they would a new customer and work to reacquire their business each day. As Tom Reilly says, "Treat your customers as if they were prospects, because they are prospects – for your competitors."[3]

The final Contractor Kool-Aid teams drink might be the most expensive of all. It's drunk by contractors who *overrate* the quality of their relationship with their customer and *underrate* the concerns and frustrations expressed by their customer. Too often I've seen this Kool-Aid cost contractors a billion dollars as they blithely march into proposals with the grandiose assumption that "the customer loves us and will assuredly be our advocate at the moment of award decision."

To avoid this happening to you, it helps to stop "guesstimating" customer relationship assessments and instead use the qualitative analytics of the Relationship Continuum.

How to Qualitatively Measure Your Customer Relationships

Years ago in Chicago, there was a campaign to reign in juvenile delinquency. The effort included a public service announcement on the local television channels. Each night the locals heard: "It's 10:00 p.m. Do you know where your children are?" Those serving customers in the government would often benefit from a similar question: "It's 10:00 a.m. Do you know where your customer is?"

To understand the true indicators of where you stand in the eight stages of the Relationship Continuum, look again at the continuum, then look in the chart below for the descriptors of each stage. Notice in particular how the tone of the relationship changes as you move from left to right on the continuum.

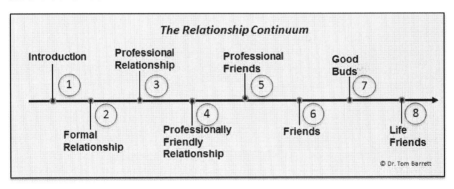

Qualitative Analytics

Stage	Tone
1. Introduction	*No real knowledge, trust, or familiarity between you and the customer.* *Your face, name, company position, and value are largely unknown.* *You are still working hard to establish rapport and find reasons*

Stage	Tone
	for future interaction.
2. Formal Relationship	*Your guard is up with "Sunday best" behavior required.* *You are polite and deferential and have little margin for fun, spontaneity, or discussion of non-business topics.* *You know each other's name, face, etc. but not much about each other beyond work.* *Trust, candor, and freedom are limited.*
3 Professional Relationship	*You are polite and cordial.* *You are viewed with increasing professional regard but have very limited personal relationship.* *You are learning to work together without learning much about each other.* *Your discussions focus almost exclusively on work-related topics.* *You have professional engagement with minimal emotional connection.*
4. Professionally Friendly Relationship	*You are more relaxed; increasing freedom to be yourself.* *It's easier to get meetings, speak on phone, get prompt answers to email, etc. Trust is increasing.* *There is a growing knowledge of each other's work style, personality and roles.* *There are increasing moments of spontaneous small talk, fun, or awareness of life beyond work.* *There is more freedom to ask non-work-related questions; discuss life events.* *You can have lunch, coffee or drinks for business meetings versus office only.*
5. Professional Friends	*First names or informal titles are used in voicemail, email, and face-to-face meetings. (At least in private meetings with customer.)* *Access is easier.* *They call you with questions they have or information you might need.* *There is solid trust, respect, and freedom to enjoy or share human moments.* *You know their hobbies, interests, and names of key people in their lives.*

Stage	Tone
6. Friends	*You have easy access and easy conversation.* *You spend some time together outside of work (grab lunch, dinner or drinks) or do non-work-related activities (sporting events, golf, etc.)* *You can call customer to just say "hello" with no agenda.* *You enjoy more laughter, share jokes and stories; increasing texts and emails for "fun" or non-work items.*
7. Good Buds	*There is genuine trust, friendship, and enjoyment of the relationship.* *Permission to call their private cell phone, at home, or in the evening.* *Staff are told to "let you through" when you call.* *Human moments of laughter, concerns, or difficulties are shared easily.* *More kibitzing, laughter, high-fives, fist pumps, and the "handshake-hug."* *Life stories are known.*
8. Life Friends	*You have deep trust and safety.* *Your relationship will outlast your work life.* *Key life moments are shared (weddings, key family events, funerals, etc.)* *You "show up" just because you care.* *You are called when life is unusually fun, exciting or difficult.* *You are a true friend, confidant, and trusted advisor.*

Take a moment and consider your customers, particularly your key customers. Use the Qualitative Analytics guide to realistically determine where you are on the Relationship Continuum with each customer. This is especially important if your organization is about to pursue an RFP with that customer. The analytics guide will help your team avoid inflated self-scoring and color-coding that organizations often give themselves on the front end of a pursuit.

When working with large organizations, I suggest that they look at their top 50 programs and carefully assess where they stand on the continuum with these critical customers. Is the relationship stuck on the left side in stages one and two? If so, why is that the case? What do they want to do to move that customer relationship to the right? From the CEO on down, what groups of individuals need to honestly embrace a mindset of intentionally pushing their relationship one or two stages to the right with their customer counterpart? If you're in an organization of 100,000 people, what do you think would happen to your customer retention and loyalty if just five thousand employees went to work every day with the mindset of moving their relationship with their customer into the middle stages of the continuum?

If you're in a mid-size or small company, these same principles apply to your organization. And their impact is equally powerful in winning, keeping and growing your customer base. Be careful to avoid drinking the Contractor Kool-Aid. Instead assess where you stand with your customers. Develop the mindset of being proactive about protecting and pushing your relationship with the customer wherever possible.

Note that I say "whenever possible." A few of your customers will not let you move the relationship one iota. They are like Steve Jobs, who when standing around waiting for a meeting to begin, was asked by a new employee, "Steve, how was your weekend?" Jobs immediately turned his back to the employee and said to others, "Let's elevate the level of this discussion." Not much margin for warm fuzzies there.

For various reasons, some customers are always serious and never let others have a human moment with them. They want to stay "in character." But for every one of those individuals, there are hundreds of others who would welcome some human moments into their professional lives.

As you develop the mindset of pushing the relationship, be aware that it's not something you can hurry or force. As a senior government official commented, "You cannot surge relationships, trust or confidence. It takes time." Typically, it requires three visits before a customer even begins to open up regarding what they really need.

It also takes tact and patience to nudge a relationship beyond stages one and two. You need to keep showing up, truly care about the customer's success, and demonstrate that you have their back and are *not* just there to take their money. Show you care. Show you have their interest at heart.

If you're in BD/Sales, after meeting with your customer, be certain to return to your office and represent the voice of your customer to your organization. Be the customer's advocate within your company.

To begin developing a mindset to "Push the Relationship," consider the four recommendations below:

1. Make a list of those you want to nudge along the Relationship Continuum.

2. Commit to follow your customers as they rotate to other assignments.

3. Practice business trip +1. Extend either end of your business trip by one day to have a meal with customers.

4. Show up. Plan one day a month at the Pentagon, or your agency, for customer visits. This forces you to lean in and make it happen.

When you lean, remember:

- "People STILL want to do business with their friends."[4]

- "The most important thing is to get to know these people as friends, not potential customers."[5]

- "Every great business is built on friendship."[6]

- "I've learned that people will forget what you said, people will forget what you did, but people will never forget how you made them feel."[7]

- "…whenever possible, work to win customers first; then work to win their business."[8]

- "It's not just about having relationships; it's about *winning because of your relationships*."[9]

---

[1] Senior Acquisition Official

[2] Garber, Peter, *101 Ways to Build Customer Relationships*. Demo, 2007. iBooks.

[3] Reilly, *Value Added Selling*, 2010, Page 140

[4] Gitomer, *Little Black Book of Connections*, 2006

[5] Ferrazzi and Raz, *Never Eat Alone*, 2005, Page 43

[6] JC Penney

[7] Maya Angelou

[8] Pugh and Bacon

[9] Carl Dickson blog; *Captureplanning.com*

Chapter 4 Become a Professional Forger

Don't be afraid to bring humanity to the world of technology.

Dr. Dave Potts is a dear friend and one of the most extraordinary people I know. He's a delightful blend of intellect, character, and competence, mingled with a terrific sense of humor. He's also a former Air Force officer with a second successful career in the defense industry.

When teaching, Dave often tells a story about growing up in Fort Worth, Texas, where his father was a paint salesman. As a young boy, he would often accompany his father on Saturday mornings as he made his rounds to various hardware stores to visit customers. His father would browse around the store, notice which paints were selling, and spend time chatting with the owner. On many occasions, his father would literally be given the keys to the store and work the cash register for the owner so he could slip away for an important event. (It was no small statement of trust from his customers to entrust him with their entire store.)

When Dave looks back on those Saturday mornings visiting customers with his father, he recognizes, "My dad was not selling paint. He was forging relationships." After sharing this quaint story from his life, Dave then explains that in the government, we too need to focus on forging relationships with our customers.

To some, the thought of forging a relationship with a customer is a foreign concept. For example, one of my favorite groups of people to work with are engineers. Without question, they are some of the smartest people on the planet tasked with solving the most daunting technical challenges in the world. But forging anything beyond a formal relationship with their customer counterpart is just not part of their mindset. When working with these individuals my advice is always, *Don't be afraid to bring humanity into the world of technology.* They, like all of us, need to remember Jim Collins' succinct insight: *Business is people.*

Similarly, Horst Schulze, the chairman and CEO of the Capella Hotel Group, implores people to let go of the notion of business-to-business and remember that business is always person-to-person. When working with the government, it too is person-to-person. One person, one conversation, one engagement at a time. One human being interacting with another human being.

The more you develop a mindset that is intentional about forging a relationship with your customer, the sooner you reap the rewards of being in stages four, five or six on the Relationship Continuum. To do this successfully, it helps to know the six habits of those who excel at relationships that win business.

Habit 1 – Stay in Style

Most of us know from experience that it's no fun to walk into an event and discover that our attire is completely out of sync with what is expected. When it comes to connecting with your customer, there are some garments that are always in style. One of them is kindness.

Colin Powell, the former Secretary of Defense and Secretary of State, is one of my favorite leaders. He tells a story about the underground parking lot at the State Department. Because the parking lot is too small for all the cars, the parking attendants line up the employees' vehicles one behind the other. At the end of the day when the employees are leaving, only those with vehicles at the head of the line can promptly drive away. The rest have to wait for the attendants to extricate their cars from the lines.

One day, Secretary Powell asked the attendants how they determine whose car gets put at the front of the line versus stuck in the line. He wondered if it was based on rank or some other process. The answer from the attendants was telling. They reported that those who enter the parking lot in the morning and take a moment to roll down their window and greet the attendants, or simply smile and wave, have an uncanny way of finding their cars at the front of the line. Those who ignore the attendants or treat them disrespectfully tend to find their vehicles snarled in the middle of the line.

It's funny how the garment of kindness is always in style and noted by others. Choose to wear it and "kill 'em with kindness" even during first encounters where the customer is sometimes unfriendly or hostile. That's why Jeffrey Gitomer reminds us:

"There is a universal truth of connecting. Your mother taught you everything you need to know about connecting before you were 10 years old: Make friends, play nice, tell the truth, take a bath, do your homework."[1]

For most of us, bathing is not typically the problem, but the other items sure are. We all need to remember Stephen R. Covey's advice that, "Little kindness and courtesies are so important. In relationships, the little things are the big things."[2]

When you show up wearing humility, courtesy and respect, it's noticed and remembered. In fact, "Courteous treatment will make a customer a walking advertisement."[3]

Habit 2 – Step into Their World

Henry David Thoreau once wrote in his diary: "The greatest compliment that was ever paid me was when one asked me what I thought, and attended to my answer." (It's ironic that we are taught to ask questions but not taught to sincerely listen to the answer.) Relationships that are valued by your customer begin when you stop telling the customer about your world and instead take the time to learn about theirs. "When you know what's going on in people's world and what's important to them, you're building a better relationship."[4]

It's impossible to develop deep understanding of your customer's world and the nuances of who they are, how they think, and what's important to them without a mindset that chooses to intentionally step into their world. It takes effort to get out of your own world and into the world of others. It takes discipline to remind yourself that the goal in the customer meeting is to: show up, shut up, and listen up.

It's particularly easy to make the classic mistake of over eagerness when contractors don't know their customers well. In their eagerness to establish credibility or impress the customer, they frontload the meeting with talk about themselves or their company's size, scope, services, locations, leadership, products, programs, blah, blah, blah. They wind up doing the proverbial *show up and throw up*. They talk too much and listen too little. And then they're confused as to why they're having difficulty getting a follow-up visit with the customer.

In the moments when you are tempted to forget what matters most to your customer, remember this piece of sardonic counsel from one of the veterans of the procurement world:

"Remember the three things the customer is interested in:

1. Themselves.

2. Er…

3. That's it.

Not understanding the buyer's locus of interest sets you up to fail."[5]

Habit 3 – Start with the Right Expectations

In our personal lives, beginning a relationship with the right expectations is a critical launch point for relationship success. Anthony Robbins, the renowned motivational guru, reminds us, "Some of the biggest challenges in relationships come from the fact that most people enter a relationship in order to get something: they're trying to find someone who's going to make them feel good. In reality, the only way a relationship lasts is if you see your relationship as a place that you go to give, and not a place that you go to take."[6]

Likewise, customer relationships are more successful when we begin with a mindset of enhancing the life of our customer. As Jeffery Gitomer notes, for some of us, "Providing value to someone is a whole new way of thinking. It means give first rather than 'ask for' first. It means helping others so that they look forward to helping you back."[7]

To clarify the importance of a mindset that wants to help customers, Burg and Mann explain the need to avoid what they call the big inversion; a complete misconception of what it means to be in sales.

"But the biggest inversion of all, the great upside-down misconception about sales, is that it's an effort to get something from others. The truth is that sales at its best that is, at its most effective-is precisely the opposite: it's about giving. Selling is giving: giving time, attention, counsel, education, empathy, and value. In fact, the word sell comes from the old English word 'sellan,' which means – you guessed it – 'to give.'"[8]

Adam Grant refers to this mindset of giving while expecting nothing in return as being *otherish*. He explains, "Being otherish (successful giver) means being willing to give more than you receive, but still keeping your own interests in sight, using them as a guide for choosing when, where, how, and to whom you give."[9]

Habit 4 – See the Sign

Mary Kay Ash was known for her core belief that everyone has an invisible sign hanging from their neck that says, "Make me feel important."

"Think back to the last time you had that really warm glow inside when somebody made you feel special because they saw a sign hanging around your neck that said M-M-F-I, or Make Me Feel Important. One of the basic principles of winning customers away from your competition is to make them feel wanted, needed, and appreciated."[10]

It isn't obvious, but government customers wear this sign. When meeting with them, watch for their M-M-F-I sign and then actively look for ways to affirm them. Remember that your task is not to impress them with how important you are. It's to have a mindset of honoring them by making them feel important about who they are and the work that they do.

Like the M-M-F-I sign, when meeting with your customer, it may help to remember the ancient proverb that says, "Pleasant words are like honeycomb, sweetness to the soul and health to the body."

When you seek opportunities to enrich the lives of your customers, you will be amazed at how much more easily you can schedule future visits with them.

Habit 5 – Stay Tuned

The brilliant leadership analyst Warren Bennis teaches that boredom is what happens when you fail to make someone interesting.

Stay tuned to the fact that every customer is a fascinating human being that you are eager to know. Let them tell you their story. Fight the desire to interrupt their narrative so you can share your story. Instead, stay silent, tune in, and enjoy the monologue.

"Don't just act interested, be interested. So: How do you master the skill of being interested – and be sincere when you do it? The first key is to stop thinking of conversation as a tennis match (he scored a point. Now I need to score a point.) Instead, think of it as a detective game, in which your goal is to learn as much about the other person as you can. Go into the conversation knowing that there is something very interesting about the person, and be determined to discover it."[11]

Habit 6 – Stay Seated

Oprah Winfrey poignantly states: "Lots of people want to ride with you in the limo, but what you want is someone who will take the bus with you when the limo breaks down."

Developing great customer relationships is easier when you model a mindset of honestly caring about your customer's life, regardless of whether or not you do any business together.

In a tough town like Washington, D.C., where friendships are completely disposable, especially if someone loses their position as a person of power and influence, this mindset quickly differentiates you from others.

There is one aspect of living in the DC area that I find psychologically fascinating: Washingtonians are not more problem free than the rest of the population. They just have more sophisticated defense mechanisms. They are very adept at hiding their problems from public view. This is particularly the case with many political and military leaders. They find that it's safer to be guarded and not allow people into their interior lives. As a result, they are individuals who are professionally friendly and personally friendless.

But, even in DC, customers value you more when they know that you are sincerely interested in their lives and that your kindness is not predicated on their successes.

To maintain a mindset of *staying seated* with customers you care about, consider two definitions of friendship:

- A friend is someone who doubles your joy and divides your sorrows.

- A friend is someone who enters stage left just as others are exiting stage right.

If you model a mindset of honest interest in your customers, whether they are riding in the limo or the bus, you will quickly differentiate yourself as a person of value.

Before reading ahead, take a moment and review the six habits that help form smart customer relationships. My guess is that you probably embrace most of them. Because let's be honest, it's tough to argue against human courtesy, being otherish, kind, or interested.

But remember, *our challenge is not embracing these behaviors. It's keeping them top of mind, front and center as a mindset that we intentionally recall and live out each day in every interaction with our customers.*

When your internal beliefs become your daily behaviors, your customer relationships change significantly. Magically, the relationships begin to slide right on the Relationship Continuum, quietly differentiating you from your competitors.

---

[1] Gitomer, *Little Black Book of Connections*, 2006, Page 41

[2] Stephen R. Covey, http://www.azquotes.com/quote/529651

[3] James Cash Penney

[4] McGee, *How to Succeed With People*, 2013, Page 192

[5] Keyser, 2014

[6] Anthony Robbins

[7] Gitomer, *Little Black Book of Connections*, 2006, Page 51

[8] Burg and Mann, *Go-Givers Sell More*, 2010, Page 1

[9] Grant, *Give and Take*, 2013, Page 158

[10] Wilson, *151 Quick Ideas to Get New Customers*, 2005, Page 21

[11] Mark Goulston , *Just Listen*, Page 59

Part Two:
The Power of
Smart People
Skills

Chapter 5
The Power of
Microbursts

Never underestimate the large impact of a small gesture.[1]

Years ago I passed Malcolm Gladwell's litmus test of 10,000 hours required for the development of proficiency and expertise. On Capitol Hill, I have spent over 10,000 hours meeting one-on-one with senators and members of Congress. I have spent thousands more hours with people in the procurement world, both contractors and government customers.

Do you want to know what I learned from all that time? Without question, these individuals are smart, gifted, and dedicated. But I have also learned something else: Like you and me, they are just people. People with hopes and hearts. People who, when appropriate, like to laugh, have fun, or drop their guard. They like to be with others who enrich their lives. They like to be with those who understand the pressures and responsibilities they are tasked to manage. They like to be with people who respect and value them. And, when they're in work mode, they're grateful for people who bring them value.

Your customers are no different from mine. They may have their game faces on and their guards up. They may have impressive positions, titles, or rank. But they are still people. And when you get serious about connecting with them as people, there is a silent but significant shift in their perception of you and the role you play in their work worlds.

So how do you learn to create this shift and connect more authentically with your customer? *Understand the Power of Microbursts.*

What is a Microburst?

Accuweather.com describes a microburst as:

"A small column of exceptionally intense and localized sinking air that results in a violent outrush of air at the ground. It's capable of producing damaging straight-line winds of more than 100 mph that are similar to that in some tornadoes, but without the tornado's rotation. A microburst often has high winds that can knock over fully-grown trees. The size of a microburst is typically less than 3 miles across, and its lifespan could range from a *couple of seconds* to several minutes."

Now, if that's more information about a microburst than you wanted, I understand, but here's the point. In weather, microbursts have two intriguing features: power and brevity. In a very brief timespan, they can have a huge impact. These same phenomena occur when you are interfacing with your customers. There are microbursts of small, seemingly insignificant customer touch points that powerfully shape your customer's connection with you. As these brief moments build up, the strength of your relationship equity grows exponentially.

Knowing how to recognize microbursts the instant they occur is a learned skill. Those who develop this skill find their customers inclined to be their advocates. Those who don't find their customers inclined to be ambivalent.

There are four specific microbursts that you can assiduously learn to watch for.

1. Microbursts of Meta-Message

Like a shooting star that quickly flames out of sight, a meta-message is a customer comment that trumps everything else that he or she says. It represents the one key point they want you to hear and grasp. On a scale of one to ten, the comment has level-ten importance to your customer.

The meta-message may be stated emphatically and repeatedly. When this occurs, it's relatively easy to spot. But many times, the meta-message from your customer is a five-second microburst in a 50-minute conversation. It's made only once and often delivered with little fanfare or emphasis. It can appear to be little more than a brief parenthetical comment thrown into the conversation. Your customer is expecting you to be astute enough to hear the statement, capture its significance, and respond accordingly.

When meeting with a customer, many contractors only listen for specifications and procurement details. Smart contractors also listen for the microburst of the meta-message. And when they find it, they know they have discovered pure gold. They also know that the customer's meta-message might never be explicitly stated in the RFP that hits the street.

For example, during one meeting, a Navy admiral casually mentioned that he had "never missed an equipment delivery to the fleet – even during the rapid pivot to the Asia Pacific." This quiet microburst was the admiral's way of making it perfectly clear: *"My legacy and reputation are important to me. Make certain that you assure me of this personal win when giving your response to the RFP."*

Some microbursts can be easily overlooked. Ron Ralston is one of the premiere orals presentation coaches in the country. While reviewing a proposal for a contractor, Ron could sense that the team lacked confidence in their message to the customer. They were not sure they were answering the mail while preparing a compliant presentation that would resonate with the customer's top priorities. So Ron asked the team to stop working on their proposal and tell him as much as they could remember about their meetings with the general who would be the key decision maker for this RFP. After much probing, the capture manager suddenly exclaimed, "I remember what the general said. He said, 'I'll tell you what I don't want. I don't want a Nunn-McCurdy breach.'" Initially, this five-second comment went unobserved. But it

---

* A Nunn-McCurdy breach occurs when a program's unit cost exceeds certain thresholds. When that happens, DoD must notify Congress of the breach. There are two types of Nunn-McCurdy breaches: significant breaches and critical breaches. A breach of the significant cost growth threshold occurs when the program acquisition unit cost or the procurement unit cost increases by at least 15% over the current baseline estimate or at least 30% over the original baseline estimate. A breach of the critical cost growth threshold occurs when the program acquisition unit cost or the procurement unit cost increases by at least 25% over the current baseline estimate or at least 50% over the original baseline estimate. The Nunn-McCurdy process has been amended a number of times over the years. For example, in the Weapon Systems Acquisition Reform Act of 2009, Congress enacted a new provision requiring the Secretary of Defense to terminate a program that experiences a breach of the critical cost growth threshold, unless the Secretary of Defense submits a written certification to Congress.

became the key to designing a winning proposal that covertly assured the general of the team's unflinching commitment to delivering an on-time, on-budget, low-risk proposal.

When looking for microbursts of the meta-message, be aware that sometimes your customer's microburst is not only swift, it's also silent. As one senior officer counseled his aide de camp:

- *Never write in a paragraph what you can write in a sentence.*

- *Never write in a sentence what you can write in a word.*

- *Never write in a word what you can speak in a paragraph.*

- *Never speak in a paragraph what you can speak in a sentence.*

- *Never speak in a sentence what you can speak in a word.*

- *And never speak in a word what you can say with a nod.*

2. Microbursts of Connection

The CEO of Zappos.com says, "Every call is perceived as a way to make a positive emotional connection with a customer." If you want to forge a smart relationship with your customer in the government space, then follow his advice. Look for occasions to have an authentic and meaningful microburst of connection with your customer. Remain alert for human moments when your customer reveals a specific desire, frustration, joy, hope, or anything else that has them emotionally engaged. These brief moments have the effect of moving your relationship with your customer to the right while also causing the customer to look forward to future brief moments with you.

Microbursts of connection with your customer don't have to be work related. They can be about sports, travel, hobbies, family, and an endless array of life events. They can be fun or funny.

Sometimes they're unexpected moments of human candor. I experienced one today while writing this chapter. To prepare for an upcoming speaking engagement in Milan, Italy, I had a 30-minute Skype call scheduled with the corporation's CEO. During our meeting, she offhandedly mentioned that her brother is in the final stages of losing his battle with cancer. Upon hearing this, I had two choices: I could ignore this discovery and get back to our business agenda, or I could pause the meeting and spend a few moments to quietly let her explain her brother's condition. I chose the latter, and we wound up having a meeting that was professionally productive while interspersed with some very real, human connection.

Brene Brown is one of the leading authorities on the topic of vulnerability. To her own surprise, her TED Talk, *The Power of Vulnerability*, has been viewed 25 million times and remains one of the top-ten TED talks in history. Why this extraordinary worldwide response? Because, she reminds us, "We are not thinking people who sometimes feel. We are feeling people who sometimes think." As human beings we long to feel heard, understood and connected to others. We want to engage with others in authentic, honest dialogue.

She also explains that the act of being vulnerable and candid with others (and ourselves) is profoundly uncomfortable for many people. They would rather show you their carefully crafted persona than reveal their real person.

As noted earlier, this is particularly the case when interacting with some customers in the government. However, if you are not afraid to bring humanity into your work world and remember to maintain a mindset of looking for microbursts of connection, you will be amazed at how often people give you glimpses into their interior worlds. And if you recognize these moments and handle them wisely, the tenor of your relationship with these individuals will quietly change to one of trust and candor.

3. Microbursts of Genuine Laughter

Once you get people laughing, they're listening, and you can tell them almost anything.[2]

When teaching at corporations that do business with the government, particularly large defense contractors, I often begin by asking two questions:

- Do you believe it's possible for someone to be rather smart and still have a sense of humor?

- Do you believe it's possible to laugh while learning?

After asking these questions there is usually some curious laughter mixed with the hope that the training might actually be enjoyable while also being highly valuable.

In the government world, most people are confused about the role and place of humor or laughter when interacting with customers. As a result, they often avoid it all together. This is a mistake. Don't lose your sense of humor. Lighthearted moments with your customer are not to be avoided; rather they should be enjoyed... *provided they are appropriate to the situation.*

Paradoxically, the value of humor and lighthearted moments is anything but light. There is nothing frivolous about well-used humor and laughter. Humor is one of the tools to help build relationships and trust. Additionally, as Stan Toler reminds us, *"Humor is to life what shock absorbers are to automobiles."* When you know how to provide a shock absorber to a customer living in the daily grind of acute stress while engaging in issues that impact the entire world, it is welcome relief. Humor lightens the mood and creates a positive vibe that allows you to connect at another level.

Notice the role and power of humor in the research below.

"Dr. William Fry of Stanford University found that in less than a half second after exposure to something funny, the whole brain, both left and right hemispheres, becomes engaged."[3]

"A study at Johns Hopkins University School of Medicine found that humor increases test scores, which means humor helps you perform better."[4]

"But new research shows that a leader's emotional style also drives everyone else's moods and behaviors – through a neurological process called mood contagion. It's akin to 'Smile and the whole world smiles with you.'"[5]

"Did you know that when you laugh and smile, your face sends signals to your brain that you are happy? Your brain literally responds to the nerves and muscles in your face to determine your emotional state."[6]

"It should come as no surprise that laughter is the most contagious of all emotions. Hearing laughter, we find it almost impossible not to laugh or smile, too. That's because some of our brain's open loop circuits are designed to detect smiles and laughter, making us respond in kind. Scientists theorize that this dynamic was hardwired into our brains ages ago because smiles and laughter had a way of cementing alliances, thus helping the species survive."[7]

"If you don't believe smiling is useful, answer these questions:

- Do you like to do business with grumpy people?
- Do you know anyone who does?

Do you think grumpy people get what they want?"[8]

On occasion, we all need to be reminded that humor is a gift. It's a natural de-stressor. Good humor literally changes the biochemistry of your brain. It releases endorphins that provide a mini-vacation and a moment of pleasure for all involved. There is a special bond that forms when people laugh together. Think of the close friends that make you laugh and how you like to be around them.

Here is a microburst of humor that an executive in the defense industry emailed to me.

The Will

Doug Smith is on his deathbed and knows the end is near. His nurse, his wife, his daughter and 2 sons, are with him. He asks for 2 witnesses to be present and a camcorder be in place to record his last wishes. When all is ready he begins to speak:

- My son, "Bernie, I want you to take the Mayfair houses."
- My daughter "Sybil, you take the apartments over in the east end."
- My son, "Jamie, I want you to take the offices over in the City Centre."
- Sarah, "my dear wife, please take all the residential buildings on the banks of the river."

The nurse and witnesses are blown away as they didn't realize his extensive holdings, and as Doug slips away, the nurse says, "Mrs. Smith, your husband must have been such a hard-working man to have accumulated all this property."

The wife replies, "The moron had a paper route."

Now I don't know about you, but this microburst of humor made me laugh out loud. It surprised my brain with an ending I didn't see coming. It gave me a mini-vacation, and it made me enjoy my relationship with this executive even more. (By the way, when your customer sends you a humorous email, it's an indicator that your relationship is not stuck on the left end of the Relationship Continuum.)

Would you like to know what I did with the joke? I took it into the U.S. Capitol and used it to kick off a leadership class that I teach to members of Congress. Then I took it to a large defense contractor and used it to start an afternoon session. Do you think these groups were offended by this lighthearted moment? Did they think it was inappropriate and unprofessional? Not a chance. They were glad for a microburst of laughter that set a positive tone for our time together.

Here is another piece of research that you might appreciate. Did you know that scientists have discovered that there is music coming out of Beethoven's grave? Yep, he's decomposing. Sorry, I couldn't help myself. This one was told to me by one the most brilliant leaders in America. Is it corny? Absolutely. But it still made me chuckle, changed my brain-state, and made me appreciate a microburst of connection with my friend via humor.

4. Microbursts of Genuine Conversation

Lobbyists, like members of Congress, are not exactly held in high regard at this moment in history, but I enjoy watching them interact with their customers. The skilled ones can spend hours playing a round of golf with a customer and then, when the moment is right, they will have a brief microburst of genuine conversation about something that is very important to them. This conversation may only last a couple of minutes, but it's the most important moment of their entire time with the customer.

When meeting with your customers, this same skill is needed. Watch for moments when it's appropriate to have a brief but genuine conversation with them.

Here are some examples and suggestions.

It was Friday just before Labor Day weekend. Renaldo was in a brutally long SDR (System Design Review) meeting with the government's technology team. At a stand up break, someone asked a general question to the group: "Are any of you doing anything fun this weekend?" As several people shared their plans, the government's chief engineer flippantly shared, "Yeah, I get to have my ticker checked this weekend." Everyone overlooked the comment except Renaldo. He caught it. He understood there might be a lot of concern buried within that glib comment. At lunchtime, he discretely went up to the customer and said, "Hey, I heard you mention what fun plans you have for this weekend. Is that a routine heart check-up or something a little more serious?" The customer then confided to him that he is in need of a pacemaker and a little stressed out about the procedure. The conversation didn't last more than a minute, but it created a shift in Renaldo's relationship with the customer that moved it to the right. As he continued to quietly show interest in his customer's health, the relationship moved from a Stage Two, Formal Relationship, to a Stage Four, Professionally Friendly Relationship. The customer became his advocate, all because of a microburst of genuine conversation about a very human moment in his customer's life.

To build government relationships, the calendar year provides several rich opportunities to create authentic microbursts of genuine conversation with your customer. When training defense contractors, here are several suggestions I make regarding the calendar.

On Memorial Day, Fourth of July, Veterans Day, Marine Corps birthday, etc., the big defense contractors spend large sums of money on television, print, and on-line ads thanking the military for their dedication and service. I applaud this, but they are missing the opportunity to have far more meaningful connections with their customers.

- For example, if you are a contractor working with the Marines, it's far more personal to create a microburst of genuine conversation with your customer by showing up unannounced at their office on the Marine Corps birthday. Stick your head in their door and say, "Hey, do you have 50 seconds? Good that's all I need. I didn't come here to discuss our program. I just wanted to stop by and thank you for your service as a Marine. Enjoy the Marine Corps birthday. See ya." Then leave. You don't even need to wait for a response.

- And you can call or send a note to current/ex-military customers to commemorate National Military Appreciation Month (NMAM) in May.

- Alternatively, let's imagine that you've been working on a tough program that has had some major challenges and some very heated moments with your customer. What would happen if, just before Labor Day, you stuck your head in their office door and said, "Hey, you got a minute? Good, I only need 50 seconds. I know that we have had some major challenges and heated moments on the program we're working together, but as we head into the Labor Day weekend, I want you to know that it's my privilege to fight and labor with you on this program. I hope you have a great holiday weekend."

- What would happen if, on July 3^{rd,} you went to a military customer without an appointment and stuck your head in the door and said, "Hey, sorry to interrupt you. Do you have 50 seconds? Good. As I get ready to celebrate this Fourth of July, I want you to know that it's not lost on me that I get to celebrate this holiday because of what you have chosen to do with your life every single day of the year. Thanks for your service. I appreciate you. Have a great weekend."

  (Admittedly, it isn't always feasible to just show up and stick your head in a customer's door. So, if necessary, find an appropriate alternative to communicate the same message in a microburst.)

Remember, looking for microbursts is a mindset. Learning to see them and knowing how to respond to them is a skill that you and your team can develop over time. You don't need to be trained as a shrink to do this. You simply need to be reminded that your customers are people. Consequently, you don't need to fear moments of connection with them. You need to lean into those moments because when you do, your relationship with your customer will move right on the Relationship Continuum. Customers will increasingly enjoy time with you, make time for you, and view you as a value-add in their worlds. Those are pretty good dividends from one skillset.

Mindset Tips:

✓ Microbursts are brief touch-points that accumulate over time into closer relationships. Microbursts are easy, but we often skip them to get down to business. Don't!

✓ People buy from people, not robots or computers. So capture their hearts and souls before their minds. Keep a 3x5-index card of customers' fears, hopes, biases, and personal connection points.

✓ It's okay to be likable and smile, laugh, and share. Until the end of time, people will buy from those they like and trust. Provide your undivided attention and ignore the ding notifications from your smartphone. TOE the mark by Turning Off the Electronics and tuning in to the customer.

[1] McGee, *How to Succeed with People*, 2013, Page 64
[2] Herbert Gardner
[3] Eklund, *The Sell*, 2015, Page 119
[4] Eklund, *The Sell*, 2015, Page 119
[5] Harvard Business Review, *On Emotional Intelligence*, 2015, Page 25
[6] Bradberry and Greaves, *Emotional Intelligence 2.0*, 2009, Page 114
[7] Harvard Business Review, *On Emotional Intelligence*, 2015, Page 31
[8] Kawasaki, *Enchantment*, 2011, Page 10

Chapter 6
The Power of
Caring

In a meeting it feels like they only want to evaluate your system. What they are really sizing up is: Do you care? Do I trust you? Do I want to work with you for years? Do you have anything to say?

What Do Customers Search For?

As a customer, the U.S. Government often has no idea how earnestly contractors work to understand the requirements described in an RFP. They are often clueless about the time, effort, and expense borne by contractors to ensure that they clearly understand the essence of an RFP. Similarly, many contractors are clueless about one innocuous phrase embedded in many RFPs released by the government. That phrase usually reads:

"While the Government SSEB and the SSA will strive for maximum objectivity, the source selection process, by its nature, is subjective and, therefore, professional judgment is implicit throughout the entire process."

Look at that phrase again. What does the government mean by *subjective*? Aren't proposals supposed to be evaluated by a team of individuals who carefully appraise each proposal based on a set of analytic criteria that intentionally eliminate subjective factors? Isn't the process designed to ensure that the best value solution and company are recognized by objective metrics and color scores?

In the ideal world, yes. In the real world, not so much.

The real world is a spreadsheet tallying *subjective* emotional scores to give the perception of objective evaluation. It's a veneer of objectivity, a false air of precision and objectivity. And it's in the phrase, "…are by nature subjective" where the value of smart customer relationships is factored in.

A senior VP from a Fortune 100 contractor regularly shares a lighthearted story that drives home this reality. He asks his organization: "Do you remember when you were in fifth grade and one day the teacher said there was going to be an election for a class officer? And then she emphatically stated, 'Now, this is not a popularity contest.' Well guess what, she lied… it's always a popularity contest."

His point is that no matter how awesome your solutions or services are, strong relationships with a customer matter, even in environments of constrained budgets, cones of silence, and commoditization. The old truism is still in play: In business, we tend to do business with those we like. And we tend not to do business with those we don't like.

When you submit a proposal to the government, whether they're evaluating your written proposal or watching your oral presentation, they're attempting to determine if they want to work with you. They have to decide if they want to walk into their future with you. And, as you will see later, it's not an inconsequential decision.

The Constant Variable: Customer Relationships

Look at the timeline graphic on the following page. It represents a high-level view of the three primary phases in the lifecycle of a program. This lifecycle can take years to develop and be repeated for decades. However, a constant variable at critical points of the lifecycle is the power of smart customer relationships. These relationships are not just one individual on the contractor side having a relationship with their government counterpart. Rather, they are an ongoing series of customer relationships involving multiple individuals in the bidder's organization and multiple individuals in the customer's organization. These ongoing relationships occur throughout the entire life of the program.

The shaded areas represent the primary customer relationship zones where there are more opportunities to build relationships. Note that Phase 1 is the most advantageous time to forge customer relationships, gain customer understanding, and position to win. Phase 2, the Proposal Evaluation, is the *Quiet Period* when relationship building and customer feedback is at its lowest point. (It's also the phase where bidders devote the vast majority of their resources, both people and new business funds.) Phase 3, is program execution when it's a constant try-out for winning the follow-on and re-competes.

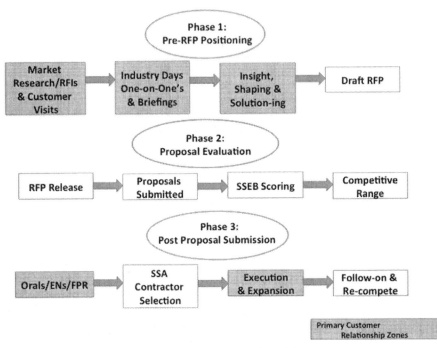

Note: EN is Evaluation Notices & FPR is Final Proposal Revision

It's expensive to buy the myth that customer relationships need to be taken seriously only by business development people in the early stages of a program and by program managers in the execution phase. In reality, every individual who has a touch point with the customer needs *a daily commitment* to the *mindset* of smart customer relationships, coupled with a relentless desire to develop the *skillsets* of effective customer relationships.

Most proposal veterans cite the number one reason for losses is lack of customer intimacy. It's useful to remember that *you are one relationship away from a win or a loss.* I have seen customer relationships that took years to develop put at risk because of one clueless team member with neither the mindset, nor skillset, of smart customer relations. I have seen billion-dollar awards lost because of contracting officers who honestly believe that skilled customer relations are irrelevant. The touchy-feely stuff of being thoughtful, choosing words skillfully, and protecting their relationship with the customer while managing contract terms, disputes, or misunderstandings was child's play to them. In their mind, the only thing that mattered was what the contract says and the terms of the agreement. In the end, they got a brand-new contract with terms that were easy to understand: *We have awarded our business with you to your competitor.*

The customer's decision to walk into their future with you culminates at the award, but the data for that decision begins being collected in Phase 1, long before the RFP hits the street. In fact, the data collection begins in earnest the moment your customer meets you or anyone else on your team

The Google Search

An easy way to understand this data collection is to look at what happens with the standard practice of a Google search. Before you visit a new customer, you try to learn and download as much as possible about the individual and their organization. You want to know who they are, what they do, and what you might have in common with them. You want to be aware of their current positions, responsibilities, and program needs. And these are just the preliminary facts you want to learn.

Of course, while you're doing a Google search on your customer, they are doing one on you. In all probability, before your arrival, they attempted to learn similar facts about you and your organization. What many people don't know is that the moment your customer meets you, they instantaneously start a second Google-type search of deep analytics.

To understand this, imagine looking into your customer's brain and seeing the Google search icon that is usually at the top of your computer screen; the spinning circle with the small gap. When spinning rapidly, it's in the process of searching and retrieving needed data. Figuratively speaking, when your customer meets you, this icon starts spinning rapidly as the brain is searching for data and information about you. This search is conscious and unconscious, intentional and intuitive. It's in-depth, intangible, and ongoing. And it's profoundly determinative of the customer's willingness to meet with you again, let alone work with you in the future.

At a rate of 350 megabytes per second, your customer's sensory receptors are scanning, processing, and synthesizing to ascertain answers to a wide array of questions. The search often begins with initial sensory hunches which can be very powerful.

For example, one contractor I worked with won a competitive award from the FBI. After the award, the program manager asked the customer, "What were the key elements of our proposal that caused you to select us?" He assumed it had to do with the team's experience, management capability or technical superiority. Consequently, the response surprised him.

The customer replied, "During your oral briefing, there was just something about the way you entered the room. You looked and acted like a team that we'd like to work with."

Amazing! Data points were gleaned before a PowerPoint was seen. And those small data points became the tipping point that resulted in a win.

Like the FBI, the instant you make contact with your customer, a data search on you begins. The customer's brain is searching for early indicators of your experience, credibility, passion, enthusiasm, or vision.

It's also scanning for initial indicators of:

LIKEABILITY – TRUSTABILITY – CAPABILITY

SINCERITY – DIVERSITY – COMPATABILITY

HUMILITY – ADAPTABILITY – AGILITY

In the Blink of an Eye

"Research performed by Princeton psychologists Janine Willis and Alexander Todorov in their article, 'First Impressions', reveals that you have the time it takes to blink an eye – that is, 1/10th of a second – before someone has made a judgment about your likability, competence, trust worthiness, and aggressiveness."[1]

At a more granular level, the customer's brain has begun a search of seemingly random but critical questions. It wants to determine your character, competence, value, and likeability. Regarding these, it's trying to ascertain:

Character:

- What kind of character do you possess?
- What are your values?
- Do I trust you?
- Are you sincere?

Competence:

- What's your level of competence?
- What's your level of experience?
- What's your area and depth of expertise?

Value and Values:

- Are you committed to my success or only your own?
- Do you want to sell me or seek to understand me?
- Are you here to impress me or to help me succeed?
- Are you here to talk *at* me, *to* me, or *with* me?
- Are you able to solve my problems?
- Are you able to bring value?
- Will time with you be valuable?

Likeability:

- Do I resonate with you?
- Do I like you?
- Will time with you be enjoyable?
- Are you someone I'd like to meet with again?
- Are you someone I'd like to work with in the future?
- Are you a team player?

What Your Customer Wants to Know About You

At a minimum, before you can build a relationship or win business, the customer wants to decipher three things about you:

1. Do you CARE?

2. Do I TRUST you?

3. Do you have anything to SAY?

Incidentally, the order of these three questions matters to your customer. They aren't inclined to listen to what you have to say until they are satisfied with their answers to the first two questions: Do you care and do I trust you? As John Maxwell reminds us: "People don't care how much you know until they know how much you care."[2]

Outcare your competitors.

Daniel Pink asks: "After meeting with you, what do you want the customer to think, feel, and do?" Note carefully his three words: think, feel, and do. Business relationships that win begin when you have absolute clarity about what you want your customer to think and feel regarding you. If you want to establish a smart relationship with your customer, begin with a mindset that says, *I want my customer to know that I care; I can be trusted; and I have something to say.*

Customer Question #1: Do You Care?

Show that you truly care.

At the zenith of her career, the country music megastar Shania Twain had a hit song entitled, *That Don't Impress Me Much.* It's a song about the various ways people try to impress others while completely ignoring the simple power of human connection. When watching government contractors interact with their customers, I often think of this song. Like a bad first date, too many contractors on their opening visit attempt to impress the customer with who they are and what they, or their company, have done. Their lead message is all about themselves while the thought-bubble of the customer is *That don't impress me much.*

There is another way to impress your customer: impress them with how much you care. Caring is defined as: "displaying kindness and concern for others." The power of caring starts with the practice of OPI, namely focusing on *Other People's Interests*. When you master the mindset of genuinely focusing on your customer's interests, it becomes much easier to get repeat visits. This is because the customer actually *enjoys,* rather than *endures* their interaction with you. Furthermore, by focusing on the customer, you learn more information about the customer's vision, values, and vicissitudes. And it's this knowledge that enables you to bring value to them in the future.

Customers also want to know if you care when it isn't just self-serving to do so. They want to know:

- *Do you care about me when there is no upcoming procurement?*
- *Can you celebrate my success even if not with you?*
- *Do you care more about me than the money?*

Sometimes, showing that you care is less difficult than expected. Larry is the CEO of a mid-sized corporation. He wanted some insights regarding his leadership style, specifically with his senior management team. I agreed to help him and made time to observe his leadership meetings. One Sunday afternoon, it occurred to me that he hadn't sent me his goals and objectives for his next-day meeting. So I sent him this email:

Larry,

Please send me the agenda for your leadership meeting tomorrow morning.

In your corner,

Tom

The next morning, Larry chaired his meeting and I made my observations. It ended at noon, and just as I was preparing to leave the headquarters, Larry called out to me, "Hey, Tom, do you have a minute? Come back with me to my office."

As we walked into his office, he immediately closed the door. Then he began speaking before either of us sat down. He said:

"Tom, this is a forty-year-old family business, and I live every day with the pressure of running this corporation. But last night, when I got your email and saw that you signed it, 'In your corner,' I felt for the first time

in years that someone else cared about the responsibility and pressure that are on my shoulders every single day." Then, with tears in his eyes, he added, "I cannot tell you how much that meant to me."

As I left his office, I was reminded how little things can turn out to have big impacts. It's easy to forget the power of small things in the high speed of daily life. Particularly those small indicators that demonstrate that we care about someone else. This is one of the reasons that Jim Collins reminds leaders "to never lose sight of the value of a word of encouragement."

All of us need reminders on occasion:

- Reminders to be interested in other people

- Reminders to stop obsessing about our own lives

- Reminders to have sincere interest in the lives of other people, especially our customers

- Reminders like that of Paul McGee, who advises: "If you want to influence other people, start by showing a genuine interest in them. But remember, if you are faking interest people will notice."[3]

And we need reminders that those who understand the importance of smart customer relations don't feign interest in the customer; they actually have a mindset of honest interest in the customer.

Customer Question #2: Do I Trust You?

Trust is the non-negotiable ingredient in successful business relationships. Customers want to know that they can trust you. They are searching and shopping for trust. As Steven Covey makes clear, trust has two components. The first is your *character*, and the second is your *competence*. Both of these must be present for trust to be granted.

Your customer's Google search for trust-ability begins the moment they meet you and continues to the last moments of contract execution. And, in the critical moment of decision when your customer decides who receives the contract award, trust is paramount. When your customer trusts your character and competence, you make it easy for them to be your advocate at award selection.

I suggest that you periodically pause to consider where you are in the trust process with your customer. Is your mission to establish trust, sustain trust, repair trust, or restore trust? Bear in mind:

- "We are all in the business of Trust Me."[4]

- Initial trust can take root quickly.

  Deep trust grows roots slowly.

  All trust can be uprooted instantly.

- "Trust is a local issue. If you want more trust in your work relationships, start with yourself. A practice of trust building is a practice of relationship building. If you want to grow trust or rebuild a broken trust, focus on building your relationships."[5]

Following are 10 ways to demonstrate that a work relationship matters.

"Trust grows in relationships when…

1) The relationships are mutually beneficial

2) When you bring the best of who you are into the relationship; the best includes core elements like integrity, tolerance, honesty, and trustworthiness

3) When you want the best for the other person

4) When the relationship is more important than any single outcome

5) When you invest time, communication, commitment, and authenticity

6) When you show genuine care, concern, and compassion

7) When you operate with appreciation, politeness, and inclusion

8) When you give more than you take, while still keeping your interests in view

9) When you help others achieve their aspirations, dreams, goals, or personal best

10) When you respect where others are coming from – knowledge, experience, state of mind, values, beliefs, needs."[6]

When is the best time to build trust with a customer and demonstrate that you care about them? It's long before you ever need anything from them. A mindset of showing genuine respect and kindness to those who have no power to help you can have amazing consequences. When training those who work on Capitol Hill or in the defense industry, I suggest they learn to "pay attention to the furniture" when visiting their customer. As Bennis recommends, I want them to "be a first class noticer."[7]

Do you want to know what happens when many contractors come to visit their customer on a military base or in the Pentagon? The contractor arrives early for the appointment, tells the personnel out front who they are waiting for, and then they take a seat and reflexively pick up their handheld and begin a digital dialogue with people who are miles away. Meanwhile, they ignore the personnel right in front of them! Unwittingly, they treat these individuals like a piece of furniture to be ignored, not a human being to be engaged.

Instead of falling into this pattern, learn to engage the people right in front of you. Ask them simple questions such as:

- *What's your name?*
- *How's your day going?*
- *How long have you been posted here?*
- *Do you like it?*
- *Where were you before being assigned here?*
- *How did you get from there to here?*
- *Where would you like to go next?*
- *Where did you go to school?*
- *Where did you grow up?*

These simple questions, when asked sincerely, go a long way to differentiate you from other contractors who came into that same office and ignored the personnel because they were too busy and too important to spend time talking to the "little people." Those who understand that *the essence of life is relationship* (E of L = R) never meet *little* people.

Instead, they have the joy of meeting *important* people everywhere they go.

An unintended consequence occurs when you do this. In the future, the very same individual sitting out front will be the senior officer you are hoping to meet. It's a wonderful moment when that now senior officer says, "You don't remember me, but I remember you. Years ago, I was an aide de camp working out front and I distinctly remember meeting you. I remember that you always took time to take an interest in me. It's nice to see you again. What gives me the pleasure of meeting with you now?" In these moments, the customer is saying that years ago they began a Google search on you. They already know that you care. They already know that they are inclined to trust you. So you can get started and tell them what you have to say.

Customer Question #3: Do You Have Anything to Say?

In conjunction with knowing that you care and can be trusted, government customers want confidence in your competence. They want to know that you have the ability to execute on any contract you are awarded.

Successful contract execution is paramount, regardless of how strong your relationship is with your customer. I stress this because when teaching Billion Dollar Mindsets, I notice that some people get skewed in two errant directions. One is believing that establishing extraordinary relationships with the customer exempts them from the need for extraordinary execution of the contract. The other is believing that providing great products or services exempts them from developing an extraordinary customer relationship. This binary thinking is a dangerous trap. In reality, smart business-winning relationships are predicated on a relentless commitment of engagement *with* the customer and execution *for* the customer. It's not an either/or proposition.

Mindset Tips:

✓ E of L = R. The power of caring starts with the practice of OPI, namely, focusing on Other People's Interests.

✓ Realize the customer's big three questions:

- Do you CARE?

- Do I TRUST you?

- Do you have anything to SAY?

✓ Be a first class noticer!

[1] Slattery, *Kill the Elevator Speech*, 2014, Page 91
[2] John C. Maxwell, *Relationships 101, What Every Leader Needs to Know* (Nashville: Thomas Nelson, 2003)
[3] McGee, *How to Succeed With People*, 2013, Page 155
[4] Bob Boylan
[5] Nan S. Russell, *Ten Ways to Cultivate Work Relationships and Grow Trust*, Psychology Today
[6] https://www.psychologytoday.com/blog/trust-the-new-workplace-currency/201309/ten-ways-cultivate-work-relationships-and-grow-trust
[7] Warren Bennis

Chapter 7
The Power of
Awareness

Almost everyone will make a good first impression, but only a few will make a good lasting impression.[1]

We live in extraordinary times. From deep space to deep water, we can ping information through secure networks in real time around the globe. We can be in Washington, D.C. and see people six thousand miles away with a high degree of accuracy.

Ironically, while being able to see people six thousand miles away with great clarity, many contractors are unable to see the person sitting six feet in front of them. They lack the ability to be aware of the customer they are trying to engage, understand, and serve. I call this the *6K Paradox.*

The *6K Paradox can be avoided* when you develop a mindset of awareness. Consider entering every customer encounter like a point guard on a basketball court. Great point guards have incredible court vision. They can see the entire court, feel the flow of the game, and anticipate the lanes that are about to open. They use their peripheral vision to give them real time awareness of what is happening right in front of them. Their awareness of what is happening on the court enables the whole team to play better.

The power to be aware, to be truly present and notice your surroundings is an ability that you too can develop. It begins by understanding three specific areas of awareness:

* *Situational Awareness*

- *Other People Awareness*

- *Self-Awareness*

Situational Awareness

Fighter pilots are taught to have situational awareness, especially when in in air-to-air combat. Most pilots are familiar with what is known as the OODA Loop. The OODA Loop is a decision-making process that was developed by Air Force fighter pilot and military strategist John Boyd. The four steps of the OODA Loop are Observe, Orient, Decide, and Act.

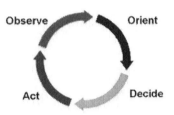

In combat, the person who can cycle through the OODA Loop fastest has the highest probability of winning. This is why there is such an enormous effort to provide our fighter pilots with full situational awareness. We want them to have complete knowledge of their environment in any situation.

This same commitment to situational awareness is practiced by those who are serious about smart customer relationships. They are constantly scanning their environment to see what is going on. They are serious about observing what is happening six feet in front of them and then acting accordingly.

When meeting with customers, get serious about becoming more observant. Practice situational awareness by considering the following questions:

- If you are giving a presentation, are you aware of the moment when the length of time you are presenting has exceeded the interest of your customer? Do you know when it's time to "dump fuel?"

- Are you aware of the subtle cues from your customer that the meeting time is expiring or that they are no longer perceiving your visit as valuable? (Many contractors who keep talking and talking remind me of a line I read on a tee shirt: *Despite the look on my face… you are still talking.*) Observe the hints!

- Are you aware that most customers have been burned by glossy brochures and rosy PowerPoint presentations that are too perfect? Are you aware that most customers would like you to skip the corporate capabilities brief? (So either trash them, put them late in your presentation, or learn to get through them in record-setting time.)

- Are you aware that many customers would like you to ditch the brief all together? They would love you to abandon your security blanket (PowerPoint) and converse at a table while only using a white board or blank sheets of paper to guide the discussion.

- Are you aware of the value of flying solo? Understand that customer candor decreases as the number of meeting attendees increases. (Think about it, do people share private thoughts with many people or are they more likely to confide in one person that they trust? Additionally, if you bring an entourage, the customer will bring theirs. Worse yet, if you bring four people and they don't, a four-on-one meeting can be awkward. It feels like a firing squad of questions.)

- Are you aware that you can talk *at, to, over, under,* or *around* people, but customers want you to talk *with* them?

- Are you aware if the customer is trying to interject a question?

- Are you stepping on and over the customer when they speak?

- Is there an introvert you need to pull into the conversation?

- Is the meeting stuck? If so, how can you fix it?

- Does the meeting need a coffee break? (Sometimes coffee breaks fuel conversation and connection more than PowerPoint.)

- Are people checking their watches, dozing off, or sitting forward and fully engaged? If they are not engaged, what are you going to do to fix it?

In combat, success depends on situational awareness. Pilots need to observe, orient, decide and act. If you want to win with your customer, your success depends on your situational awareness. Learn to make it a mindset you practice in every customer engagement.

Other People Awareness

Walk in the other person's shoes. Know the other person's agenda and help them accomplish it.[2]

Becoming aware of who you are interacting with is not difficult. You don't need to be a psychologist or a trained security expert to know how to read subtle facial expressions, hand movements, and body positions. The information you need to understand someone is clearly visible if you remember to look for it. Make it your priority to open your eyes and ears when you meet your customer.

Start by remembering that in the FAR-based world of government acquisition, it is people, not agencies, who buy. People are hoping you have the ability to be aware of a number of concerns. They are wondering:

- *Do you really understand me?*
- *Do you know my world?*
- *Have you read my mail?*
- *Have you walked down my hallways?*
- *Do you understand my requirements at the visceral level?*
- *Have you lived a day with my calendar of meetings?*
- *Do you know the pressures I receive from my customers?*
- *Do you understand the political pressures of my job?*
- *Do you know the pain of being sequestered while evaluating proposals – on top of my day job?*

One underdog client pursuing a large public safety radio contract needed to know how a police radio worked and where it was deficient. So the sales and systems engineers did a ride along with the police to develop a true awareness of the customer's world. They saw the problems, lived the pressure, and felt the pain.

After being awarded the contract, the customer said, "When listening

74

> *to you it became clear that you understood our world. It was as if you were in the squad car with us. Your solution fit like a tailor-made suit."*
>
> *That is the power of Other People Awareness.*

When meeting with your customers, have clear objectives about what you want to observe or learn in the first 30 seconds of a customer encounter. For example, do you want to immediately memorize your customer's name or become aware of his or her personality, commmunication, or leadership style?

You can predetermine to:

- *Be aware of customer wants – uncover their hopes, fears, biases and what they care about.*

- *Be aware of what the customer can buy within budget, schedule and other constraints.*

- *Be aware of the customer's buying process.*

- *Be aware of the customer's buying problem. Put yourself in his or her shoes. Think what's best for the government.*

- *Be aware of what inspires them to come to work in the morning. What are their hot buttons, personal passions, and desired personal wins?*

- *Be aware of how you can provide value to them.*

Self-Awareness

You have to exude enjoyment and enthusiasm for what you do and treat the customer like a friend.[3]

When coaching leaders privately or speaking to teams on leadership, I always encourage leaders to pay attention to what they *fill the room with*. Self-aware people want to know if they are filling the room with toxic behaviors that poison the environment or something far more positive and powerful. Lack of awareness in this critical area has cost many individuals a promotion and many bidders awards that they should have won.

Before your next meeting, take a moment and consider two questions. First, what do I want to fill the room with? Second, what am I actually filling the room with? (Many people are shocked at the difference between their answers to those two innocuous sounding questions.)

Instead of bringing a toxic mindset and behaviors to a meeting, I suggest people make a conscious effort to bring S.P.I.C.E. into their meetings. Make a point of bringing a disposition of: *Sincerity, Passion, Interest, Curiosity, and Enthusiasm*

Those who are serious about building smart customer relationships are also smart enough to understand the importance of self-awareness. They don't want to be clueless about how they are being perceived by others, especially their customers. And they certainly don't want to be diagnosed with the fictitious disease that is cleverly described below.

"Ever known anyone for years and then realized you know lots about them but they actually know very little about you?

Ever asked anyone about his or her weekend but they have never thought to ask you about yours?

Ever met someone who continually finishes off your... sentences for you... often incorrectly?

Ever worked with someone who has an annoying habit of talking over people in team meetings and who you are convinced has never really listened to anyone but themselves in their entire life?

Ever met someone who seems very insightful about everyone but themselves?

You have?

Then you have probably met someone suffering from S.A.D.S. = Self-Awareness Deficiency Syndrome. Of course, the very nature of this condition (which is not an official medical term) means the person suffering from it is entirely unaware of the fact. They are oblivious to their behavior.

They have no realization of the impact their behavior is having on others."[4]

Avoid the "Me Monster"

Steve Rubel, from the PR firm, Edelman, explains that the most important currency anyone can give you is their attention. It's worth more than money, possessions or things.

While acknowledging the wisdom of his counsel, it's easy to forget to actually practice it. It's far easier to get consumed with the "Me Monster."

To get a brilliant yet funny reminder of what a me monster sounds like, I suggest you Google, "Brian Regan Me Monster." Watch his clip about the person who is so full of himself that all he can talk about is me, myself, and I. It's a spot-on reminder of how much we all dislike being trapped with people who relentlessly draw attention to themselves.

Customers take no pleasure in visits from contractors who are full of the me monster mindset.

"When trying to connect with others, you have to remember that it's not *all* about you. Audiences detest arrogance and self-centeredness. They evoke the same feeling you get when you arrive at a party only to be cornered by a dreadful, self-centered know-it-all. He'll talk about his own interests, how cool he is, and how great he is while you're left thinking, "What an ass," and looking for any opportunity to get away. Why is that? It's because the conversation doesn't include you, your ideas, or your perspective. Self-centered people don't connect."[5]

(If you would like a fresh reminder in the art of conversation, go to www.communicationguys.com and download the free eBook, *How to Become the Person Everyone Wants to Talk To*.)

To practice the mindset of attention to others, note the clever conversational cautions from Debra Fine. She suggests be aware of:

- *"The <u>FBI Agent</u> – Assails the other person with an onslaught of questions, in an interrogation, not a conversation.*

- *The <u>Braggart</u> or Braggarita – Talks endlessly about his or her exploits.*

- *The <u>One-Upper</u> – Can't wait to top someone else's story. 'Did you like Kilimanjaro? I liked Everest more.'*

- *The <u>Monopolizer</u> – Talks without letting others have a turn. To avoid becoming a monopolizer, don't talk for more than five minutes.*

- *The Interrupter – Focuses on making his or her point, and is too impatient to let others finish making theirs.*

- *The Poor Sport – Refuses to engage in chatting. Answers open-ended questions with show-stopping one-word answers: 'Are you enjoying the conference?' 'No.'*

- *The Know-It-All – Not interested in anyone's opinions, because he or she has it all figured out."*[6]

Summary

Customers are grateful for advanced technology that enables them to accurately see events six thousand miles away. But they are desirous of contracting partners who can see their life pressures and priorities while sitting six feet across from them.

At your next meeting, watch out for the *6K Paradox*. Go into it ready to engage in situational awareness, other people awareness and self-awareness. Your customers will notice.

Mindset Tips:

✓ Like a fighter pilot, use the OODA Loop.

✓ Like a point guard, see what is unfolding right in front of you.

✓ Remember: *Eyes that look are common. Eyes that see are rare.*

✓ Watch out for the Me Monster.

---

[1] Sonya Parker
[2] Sobel
[3] Sobel, *Making Rain*, 2003, Page 174
[4] McGee, *How to Succeed with People*, 2013, Page 18
[5] Duarte, *Resonate*, 2010, Page 18
[6] *"The Fine Art of Small Talk,"* Debra Fine

Part Three: The Power of Smart Listening

Chapter 8
Develop a Mindset
to Listen

Calvin Coolidge once said, *"No one ever listened themselves out of a job."* No one ever listened themselves out of a sale, either.[1]

Imagine that you're in a new job and preparing for your first meeting with a key customer. You're excited and anxious because you definitely want the meeting to go well. You want to prove that you are a value-add to your organization. To increase your probability of success, you approach several seasoned pros in your organization, people who have been interacting with customers for years, and you ask them, "What's your best advice to ensure I have a great first meeting with one of our strategic customers?"

I ask this question when I speak to organizations about smart customer relationships. The question always evokes a variety of solid answers. Inevitably, someone says, "Listen to the customer." Hearing this I get excited and say, "Oh, that's good. Let me write that down." And then I act confused and ask five more questions:

1. *Why does it matter that I listen to the customer?*

2. *What should I listen for?*

3. *How do I know if I'm hearing what the customer wants me to hear?*

4. *How do I know if I'm a skilled listener?*

5. *How do I develop a mindset to listen?*

We'll address all of these questions, but for now, let's look at the last one. What does it mean to develop a mindset to listen?

Develop the Mindset to Listen

If we were supposed to talk more than we listen, we would have two tongues and one ear.[2]

Norm Augustine, former CEO of a Tier 1 firm, was spot on when he stated: "We've all heard the criticism he talks too much. When was the last time you heard someone criticized for listening too much?"

At the corporate level, listening is easy to embrace as part of the Mission Set. But when it comes to the daily mindset of every team member, listening is easy to forget about altogether.

Ironically, when it comes to listening, our experience can get in the way of our effectiveness. Some of us have met so often with customers that we begin to wing our time with them. We have full confidence that we will *know* what to do when the interchange begins. So we plan less, wing it more, and barely notice the subtle erosion of our listening effectiveness.

Forgetting to listen well is expensive, particularly in meetings with people that are high profile, influential, and very busy.

One of the Tier 1 defense contractors learned this the hard way. They wanted a meeting with the Chairman of the Senate Armed Services Committee so they asked the senator's chief of staff to arrange a meeting. He agreed and set it up.

On the day of the meeting, the contractor showed up with six people in tow. After being escorted into the senator's private office they sat down with the chairman and his chief of staff. Following brief introductions, this group of high-level, seasoned corporate heads were off and running. They had a presentation that was well-prepared and supported with great graphics. To ensure they respected the senator's time they began their presentation promptly and spoke swiftly. They got on a roll and were in the zone. In fact, they got into such a great flow that when the senator interrupted them to ask a question, they told him they would answer his question at the end. When he asked a second question, he was given the same sage advice. At which point, the senator folded his hands and waited for this splendid presentation to end.

When the presentation ended, the contractors asked, "Senator, do you have any questions?" He smiled graciously and said that he had no questions. Then he stood, shook each of their hands, and thanked them for coming by.

What do you think this entourage wrote on their trip report regarding the success of their meeting? In their minds the meeting went splendidly. Plus, they had proof points to justify their confidence. After all, they ended the meeting on time, they got through their entire presentation, the senator had no questions (which indicates they were exceptionally clear and cogent that day), and he thanked them for coming by.

Unfortunately, the senator did not share their views. The moment they were all out the door, he turned to his chief of staff and exclaimed, "Don't you ever let those *#%! in here again!"

What happened? These seasoned pros went into a critical meeting with a casual state of mind. In the excitement of sharing their message, they forgot to listen. Not only did they avoid Norm Augustine's counsel to listen too much, they avoided listening at even a minimal level. They ignored the senator's direct questions, missed his non-verbal cues, and had no clue what he was thinking and feeling about them. They left feeling like rock stars. The senator thought they had rocks in their heads.

But let's cut them some slack, we all make the same mistake at times. It's easy to forget, "The most important words that will ever pass between you and your prospective customers are the words spoken by them – not by you."[3]

Smart listening is rarely an accident. It is the by-product of a mind that is harnessed, focused, and intentional in every interaction. It starts with a framework that is pre-determined before the customer engagement begins.

Following are some key ideas that have profoundly helped individuals and teams resurrect their conscious commitment to extraordinary listening. (These ideas have also won them billion-dollar customers who've become their advocates.) My suggestion is for you, your team, and your organization to be familiar with all of them. Memorize some of them. And before every critical meeting, select one of them to keep top of mind while you are present with your customer.

Remember the "Dos and Don'ts"

While teaching a recent course on customer relationships, a government acquisitions officer was in my class. He offered succinct insights to make your meetings with government customers valuable to them while also differentiating you from the competition. He suggested *Seven Dos and Don'ts* of great customer meetings.

Don't:

1. *Be pushy*

2. *Begin with "how great we are slides"*

3. *Keep saying "what we can do for you"*

4. *Act like you already know what they need*

Do:

5. *Listen*

6. *Be humble*

7. *Ask open-ended questions*

In short, he was saying, "Stop the *sell and tell*. Start the *listen and learn*." Listen with the intent to understand.

Without a predetermined mindset bent on listening, it's easy to forget to heed his cautions. Over the years, I've been asked to review countless meeting agendas, slide decks, and presentations of government contractors preparing for critical meetings with a customer. And countless times, I've seen these contractors violate every one of these seven suggestions.

If you're wondering how you or your organization are doing regarding these dos and don'ts, I suggest you begin by looking at your standard corporate presentation for customer meetings. Print out the presentation in hard copy and put it on your wall. Now look at the deck and pay close attention to your opening slides. Are they about you or the customer? How long before the customer sees your how-great-we-are slides, telling them about your company's locations, size, services, products, and customers? How long before customers get the thrill of looking at pictures of the key personnel in your org chart? (By the way, when was the last time you showed a customer your org chart and the customer leaned forward with rapt attention and asked you to slow down so they could fully enjoy the thrill of your org chart? My guess is that it has been a while.) Finally, when does the customer learn of your genuine desire to listen, ask questions, and understand their realities?

If you want to differentiate yourself from five other contractors that visited your customer the same week as you, do something different: Don't ask the customer to listen to your points. Instead, make a point of listening to your customer. Remember, the best business presentation is the one you never give.

"Psychologist Dr. Joyce Brothers said, 'Listening, not imitation, may be the sincerest form of flattery.' Whenever you don't pay attention to what others have to say, you send them the message that you don't value them. But when you listen to others, you communicate that you respect them. Even more, you show them that you care. A mistake that people often make in communicating is trying very hard to impress the other person. They try to make themselves appear smart, witty, or entertaining. But if you want to relate well to others, you have to be willing to focus on what they have to offer. Be impressed and interested, not impressive and interesting."[4]

Don't just be interested. Be *more* interested. Don't just be more interested. Be *most* interested. Customers will notice.

Remember, "Listening is wanting to hear."[5] It's not waiting to talk. To listen well, note the following listening reminders:

"To increase your understanding of others as you listen, follow these guidelines offered by Eric Allenbaugh:

1. Listen with a head-heart connection.
2. Listen with the intent of understanding.
3. Listen for the message and the message behind the message.
4. Listen for both content and feelings.
5. Listen with your eyes – your hearing will be improved.
6. Listen for others' interest, not just their position.
7. Listen for what they are saying and not saying.

8. Listen with empathy and acceptance.

9. Listen for the areas where they are afraid and hurt.

10. Listen, as you would like to be listened to."[6]

"When you fail at listening, you're sending out an armada of negative messages. You're saying:

- I don't care about you.
- I don't understand you.
- You're wrong.
- You're stupid.
- You're wasting my time.
- All of the above.

It's a wonder people ever talk to you again."[7]

Stay Out of the Spotlight

Practicing good listening skills draws people to you. Everyone loves a good listener and is attracted to him or her. And if you consistently listen to others, valuing them and what they have to offer, they are likely to develop a strong loyalty to you, even when your authority with them is unofficial or informal.[8]

An effective way to practice good listening skills is to determine, prior to meeting with your customer, to stay out of the fight – the fight for the spotlight.

In group communication, there is an ever-present "fight for the spotlight." To understand this, picture in your mind a spotlight in the ceiling of your meeting room. Now imagine that spotlight is on a swivel so anyone can reach up, grab it, and put it directly on themselves. If you watch carefully, you will witness an ongoing fight for the light. You will see one person grab the light and then make a suggestion, share a thought, or proffer a major idea. The instant he or she is done speaking, a second person will grab the spotlight and put it on themselves. They will throw out their thoughts while completely ignoring or dismissing what was said by the first person. When they stop speaking, a third person will repeat the process, and so on.

Have you ever been to a meeting where multiple people are talking on multiple topics while nothing productive seems to be accomplished? You are watching a fight for the light. Watch closely and you will see how exhausting it is for people to be in meetings where many are talking but few are communicating. (There is only one thing I know that is more energy sapping than one of these poorly run, chaotic meetings. It's being trapped one-on-one with an individual who's a communication ball-hog. They grab the spotlight and then talk and talk and talk, and no one knows how to shut them up.)

"Another description for this 'conversation hog' is conversational narcissism, a term first used by Charles Derber to designate ways that American conversationalists act to turn the topics of ordinary conversations to themselves without showing sustained interest in others' topics."[9]

This fight for the light occurs thousands of times every day – in customer meetings, engineering design meetings, leadership meetings, and between groups of friends and couples. Without conscious awareness, people are in an ongoing battle to put themselves in the spotlight so their opinions can be heard or valued.

Go into your next customer meeting with a mindset to fight for the light, but don't fight to put the spotlight of attention on you or your company. Instead, consciously fight to keep the spotlight of focus and attention singularly on your customer. When the customer gives you the floor (or the metaphorical spotlight) to speak, be brief. And then intentionally return to listening, asking smart questions, and gathering insights to better understand your customer. Be relentless in your mindset to talk less and listen more. Your customer will think you're a fabulous conversationalist and will be far more amenable to meeting with you in the future. Consider using the following simple formula: "Talk about them. Talk about you. And *always* bring it back to them."[10]

If you shine the light away from yourself, "You'll uncover a glaring paradox: *The more you subsume your desire to shine, the more you will shine in the other person's eyes.*"[11]

"If your objective is to make people feel like a million bucks in your presence, you'll score a bull's-eye. You already know how to do it – on a first date, on a sales call, in a meeting with your boss. From now on, it's a matter of remembering to *do it all the time.*"[12]

Go Low Tech for High impact

C.S. Lewis, the brilliant writer and Oxford don, noted that most of us don't need instruction, we just need reminders. In the near future, wearable technology, which is finally getting serious traction in the market place, will provide us the reminders we need. Imagine being able to glance at a piece of your apparel or through the lens of your glasses and see a holographic image providing you with customer focus memory joggers. The technology will enable you to remain visually focused on your customer while you also see important reminders of skillful behavior.

Since the arrival of this technology is fast approaching, we might as well begin to identify the reminders we want to see when meeting with customers. These reminders don't need to be long or detailed. In fact, they are better when they are extremely brief. Your brain, once it's reminded, knows all the details behind a simple trigger word or phrase. Following are some memory joggers you might want to load into your wearable technology.

- *It's Not About You!* (This is a not-so-subtle reminder to stop talking about yourself!)

- *SNL* (No, this doesn't stand for *Saturday Night Live*. It's a reminder to Shut up, Notice, and Listen.) As Dave Kerpen points out, "The secret to getting people to adore you is to shut up and listen."[13]

- *W.A.I.T.* (For the impetuous talker, they occasionally need to ask themselves, "Why Am I Talking?")

- *WIIFM* (This jogger reminds you to dial into your customer's favorite radio station: What's In It For Me?)

- *Smile* (No kidding! Some of us need to be reminded to smile when talking to the customer.)

- *Be Nice* (Another no kidding memory jogger. Some of us need to remember to be nice to others, especially when having the proverbial bad-hair day.)

- ***T.O.P.*** (This jogger, like an NFL scoreboard, reminds us to watch the time of possession. Let your customer have the vast majority of time to talk.)

- ***Be Curious*** (This jogger reminds us to ask smart questions with a discovery mindset rather than trying to show the customer how smart we are.) Continue to probe and have an insatiable curiosity. As the philosopher J. Krishnamurti points out, "If you are **listening to find out**, then your mind is free, not committed to anything; it's very acute, sharp, alive, inquiring, and therefore capable of discovery."[14]

Admittedly, this use of wearable technology isn't yet available to us as consumers. So allow me to make another suggestion: Go low tech for high impact. Before you enter a meeting, write down on a 4x6 card a few key mindsets or behaviors that you want to keep top of mind during your meeting. Then place the card somewhere that allows you to discreetly glance at it during your meetings. This simple practice is unexpectedly powerful. It's quietly used by many of the most influential business, political, and military leaders in the world. Join them, and you'll be surprised at its value.

By the way, your mind will instantly identify the memory joggers that are most valuable to you. You know those behaviors that you need to apply but easily forget. Those that don't come naturally to you. Those that minimize your effectiveness unless you make a conscious effort to remember them.

Here is one last memory jogger: At your next meeting: Give the customer the SPOTLIGHT! You bring a SEARCH LIGHT.

[1] Bosworth and Zoldan, *What Great Salespeople Do*, 2012, Page 135
[2] Mark Twain
[3] Burg and Mann, *Go-Givers Sell More*, 2010, Page 161
[4] Maxwell and Dornan, *How to Influence People*, 2013, Page 62
[5] Maxwell and Dornan, *How to Influence People*, 2013, Page 71
[6] Maxwell and Dornan, *How to Influence People*, 2013, Page 72-73
[7] Goldsmith, *What Got You Here Won't Get You There*, 2007, Page 86-87
[8] Maxwell, *Relationships 101*, 2003, Page 46
[9] Slattery, *Kill the Elevator Speech*, 2014, Page 120
[10] Slattery, *Kill the Elevator Speech*, 2014, Page 124
[11] Goldsmith, *What Got You Here Won't Get You There*, 2007, Page 156
[12] Ibid
[13] The Art of People, Dave Kerpen
[14] *How to Wow: Proven Strategies for Selling Your [Brilliant] Self in Any Situation*, by Frances Cole

Chapter 9
Raise Your Listening
Levels

Be a good listener. Your ears will never get you in trouble.[1]

"It's a luxury to be understood." With this thought, Ralph Waldo Emerson captured a universal desire. Everyone wants to be understood. People want to experience being heard, listened to, taken seriously, and understood at more than a surface level. They want someone to invest the time and energy to carefully listen to them while they speak. When you do this with your customer, it immediately separates you from the competition for two reasons. First, your customer increasingly values time with you. Second, you collect insights that the competition is missing.

Let's go back to second grade and remember how to listen in two easy steps:

1. Stop talking about yourself.

2. Ask others questions about themselves.

The capacity to listen skillfully, to truly hear and understand what a customer is saying, is more challenging than it appears, especially if you want to become an astute listener. Like the game of golf, listening looks like it should be ridiculously easy but is actually maddeningly difficult.

Daniel Pink reminds us that we have not made much progress in the focusing on this invaluable skill.

"Mortimer Adler, the American Philosopher, wrote thirty years ago, 'Is anyone anywhere taught how to listen? How utterly amazing is the general assumption that the ability to listen well is a natural gift for which no training is required. How extraordinary is the fact that no effort is made anywhere in the whole educational process to help individuals learn to listen well.'"[2]

Skillful listening is a competence that all of us can develop. To know where you are in your listening competencies, look at the four listening levels.

Level 1. Pseudo Listening

Level 2. Easy Listening

Level 3. Smart Listening

Level 4. Astute Listening

Level 1 – Pseudo Listening

Boredom is having to listen to someone talk about himself when I want to talk about me.[3]

Pseudo listening is non-listening. It's been said that God gave us two ears and one mouth; maybe it's because listening is twice as hard as talking. It reminds us of the comedian who quipped, "My wife said that I don't listen... at least, I think that's what she said."

Not long ago, I was asked to play golf with one of the famous talking heads from national television. At the end of our round, after I'd developed some rapport and comfort with him, I asked, "What's it like for you to sit with all the other pundits pontificating about the national issues? Do you ever grow tired of listening to them?" Without skipping a beat, he replied, "That's easy. I never listen when they're talking. I only listen when I'm talking." My thought bubble was, *Wow, what an arrogant mindset.* This pundit exemplifies pseudo listening. He reminded me of Slattery's advice, "Remember to have a real conversation and connect with someone as a human being instead of as a walking, talking, and arrogant 'all-about-me' jerk."[4]

Pseudo listening occurs when we pretend to listen or feign interest in what another person is saying when in fact our minds are miles away. We all do it on occasion, and it's not necessarily wrong in some instances. And let's face it, when you're with a conversational ball-hog who talks incessantly while being certain that you're enthralled with his or her monologue, it's easy to tune out, particularly if they're talking incessantly about an inane subject in which you have zero interest. Some people reduce us to pseudo listening, but we *do not* have the prerogative of pseudo listening when we are with our customers.

Level 2 – Easy Listening

Easy listening is casual listening. It occurs when we are relaxed and simply following the general flow of a conversation. We track the topic, listen to the big points, and jump in and out of the narrative if we feel like it. This is the listening mode of most people during the day, and it's perfectly appropriate in many situations. It can be fun, satisfying, and it allows our brain to remain in an energy-conservation mode because we are exerting no mental effort to hear anything but the surface content of the conversation. We are not attempting to pick up on anything other than that which is inherently obvious and explicitly stated.

When it comes to our customer, easy listening has significant limitations. If we're only listening at this level, we're likely to miss the fast, subtle, and critical moments in the customer's communication. Do you recall the Southwest Airlines commercial with the line, "Life comes at you fast, want to get away?" Meaningful communication with your customer comes at you fast and you need listening skills that enable you to detect the messages they are sending. If you don't, they will send you away. To succeed in business-winning relationships, you need all people involved with customer touch points to be able to move well beyond easy listening to the next listening level.

Level 3 – Smart Listening

If you're a Washingtonian and involved in the political world, you know that the inaugural balls, inaugural parade, and the swearing-in ceremonies for a new president are a big deal. Every four years, thousands of people from around the world gather to witness this unique moment in American politics. What many of them don't know is that while they are walking around the National Mall, there are other people casually walking around doing far more than meets the eye. They are Secret Service agents wearing biological and radiation detection devices under their coats.

Smart listeners are like this, they enjoy meeting with customers and readily engage in easy listening. However, beneath their casual exterior, they are monitoring more than just the surface content of the dialogue. Their minds are working and scanning to detect the subtle comments, cues, and clues emanating from the customer. They are listening hard – not hardly listening. They know that the customer has things hidden in plain sight that they want the contractor to see, hear, feel, and sense so that the contractor can help them resolve their challenges and solve their problems.

Level 4 – Astute Listening

Astute listening is similar to smart listening, but on steroids. Astute listening is:

- The ability to hear and understand what is stated, inferred, hinted at, and alluded to by your customer.

- The ability to detect and respect your customer's values and visions, priorities and pressures.

- The ability to comprehend what the customer wants you to intuitively grasp without having to say a word.

In short, *astute listening is the ability to hear what is undetectable to others.* Like a highly trained drug-sniffing dog, people with this skill are keenly aware of their customers in ways that completely elude their less observant competitors.

This skill allows you to gather intelligence that is unavailable in the public domain. You get this intel, not because you did anything illegal or inappropriate, but because you developed the skill of hearing, observing, questioning, and understanding.

Astute listening enables you to hear the customer's subtle hints. Hints about their off-the-record priorities, concerns, or needs. Hints about your need to adjust your approach, focus, or understanding of the customer. There is pure gold in the subtle hints – if you're astute enough to detect them.

This skill is attainable to most people, but it's not easy. Before I describe the formula for astute listening, let's entertain some quotes to open up to the right mindset.

- "Danger is when your mouth operates faster than your brain." (from a wine coaster)

- "Don't talk unless you can improve the silence." Jorge Luis Borges

- "To seduce almost anyone, ask and listen to his opinion." Malcolm Forbes

- "I don't care how much a man talks, if he only says it in a few words!" Josh Billings[5]

- "I know that you believe you understand what you think I said, but I'm not sure you realize that what you heard is not what I meant." Robert McCloskey

- "My job is to talk; your job is to listen. If you finish first, please let me know." Harry Herschfield.

- "Oh, I'm sorry… did the middle of my sentence interrupt the beginning of yours?" (From a wine coaster)

Six Suggestions for Astute Listening

The basics of astute listening start with staying in the moment, looking eye-to-eye, and empathizing with the person speaking to you. Use these six more advanced suggestions to assist you with this vital skill. (Note: The first two will be discussed in this chapter and the last four in the following chapter.)

1. Check your Mindset: Plan to Listen.

"Dale Carnegie, author of *How to Win Friends and Influence People*, advised, 'You can make more friends in two weeks by becoming a good listener than you can in two years trying to get people interested in you.' Carnegie was incredibly gifted at understanding relationships. He recognized that people who are self-focused and who talk about themselves and their concerns all the time rarely develop strong relationships with others."[6]

Plan to listen and become comfortable with the "gaps."

"And people rarely tell you the whole story. They leave gaps. If you don't listen well and don't ask questions you're not getting the whole picture. That can lead to problems.

To listen really well our attitude and starting point should be *"tell me more"* rather than *"here's what I think."* Remember, sometimes it's not about "us," it's about "them." If you want people to open up, to tell you more, to get to the heart of the issue you need to listen.

Develop "the gift of the gap." Yes, that's right, "gap," not "gab." Allow people space. Don't feel the need to fill every silence. Gaps in conversation are okay. They allow the other person time to clarify and articulate their thoughts.

If I'm angry, listen. If I'm upset, listen.

If I'm excited, listen. If I'm gutted, listen.

Sometimes I don't always want or need a solution. Sometimes I'm not after an opinion. I just need to be heard. To be understood. To be listened to."[7]

2. Turn on Your Sensors

It's not just what you learn by listening that is important, it's what you say by listening that is important.[8]

If you ever get the opportunity to spend time with one of the F-35 fighter jet pilots, jump on it. I promise that you will find their professional pride, passion, and fighter pilot swagger compelling. And learning about the capabilities of this aircraft is literally beyond anything most of us have ever imagined. It still blows me away.

Imagine that your corporation's electronic sensors were on the F-35. If you had a chance to speak with the pilots immediately after they returned from a dangerous congested threat mission, what would you do if you asked them, "How did your electronic sensors work?" and they sheepishly replied, "We don't know how to tell you this, but, ah… we forgot to turn them on." My guess is that you'd be incredulous. You cannot imagine that a brilliant and highly trained F-35 fighter pilot would forget to turn the electronic sensors on.

This is exactly what happens when contractors visit their customers. These brilliant and highly trained experts often forget to turn on their sensors before going into critical meetings. They forget to focus on the customer, shut up, listen astutely, and gather intelligence and understanding.

Remember:

"The person you're talking with wants you to listen. You've heard about people that talk too much. You never heard about a person who listens too much."[9]

"You must program yourself to listen intently. It's what the Quakers call devout listening. Most people do not listen with the intent to understand. Most people listen with the intent to reply."[10]

"Listen First. Listen before you speak. Understand. Diagnose. Listen with your ears – and your eyes and heart. Find out what the most important behaviors are to the people you're working with. Don't assume you know what matters most to others. Don't presume you have all the answers – or all the questions."[11]

"You must watch and listen to your customer as sensitively and intently as military spy equipment monitors enemy movements and communication. Like the most sensitive of receptors you must be on high receive. Let nothing get by you; even the casual, offhand remark may offer clues. The three most important words in the Rainmaker's mind are 'listen, listen, listen,' and to do so on 'high receive.'"[12]

Here are a few guidelines to keep you on high receive:

- Listen, be humble and don't just wait for your turn to talk.

- As Miller Heiman suggests, pause to create three seconds of "Golden Silence." This pause lets the customer expound on open-end questions. It may seem like a long awkward pause, but it's not.

- Have your sensors on and your emotional filters off.

As you turn on your sensors, remember what to listen for:

- Data, dates, deadlines, facts, or funding (These are the easy listening starters.)

- Topics that matter to the customer

- The customer's frustrations

- The customer's hopes

- The customer's dreams and visions

- The customer's personal goals and wins

- The customer's problems, pressures, priorities, and political landscape

- The customer's agenda

  - Stated agenda

  - Hidden agenda

  - Hinted agenda

  - Avoided agenda

- Watch the oscilloscope of the customer's voice inflections! When the customer's voice spikes with brief, forcefully stated comments like, "That's right! Yes! Exactly! Absolutely! That's it!" they are telling you that you're absolutely in the target area of a topic that matters greatly to them. These are huge pieces of information they are spontaneously giving you, even if they are unaware of it.

- Turn on your sensors by noting and matching your customer in body alignment, voice volume, energy, etc.

- Watch the non-verbal cues. A classic example is television appearances of prisoners of war during the Viet Nam war. The American POWs were cleaned up and put on national television to confirm that they were being treated well and not tortured. However, while Jeremiah Denton answered questions and reported that he was being well cared for, he feigned trouble with the blinding television lights and started to blink repeatedly. He was, in fact, blinking the letters T.O.R.T.U.R.E in Morse code – confirming for the first time to U.S. Office of Naval Intelligence that American POWs were in fact being tortured. His message was "hidden in plain sight." On the occasions when your customer communicates a non-verbal message to you, even though they ostensibly said nothing, it's incumbent on you to detect the message.

- Wear your "Smart Skin." (Smart skin is made of tens of thousands of micro-sensors placed on the surface of an aircraft. Each sensor is no bigger than a grain of rice. Most interesting, these sensors are capable of *receiving* critical data, but they cannot transmit anything.)

Customers sometimes think they can't communicate important information to you because they fear a violation of fairness to other competitors. In these moments, they will often use *mitigated speech.* Mitigated speech is a form of communication that uses hints and veiled suggestions rather than forthright, candid language. These hints are hidden in quiet suggestions, a silent gesture, or facial expression. Once again, the challenge is for the listener to detect the important message stated oh-so-gently.

Malcolm Gladwell brilliantly portrays the consummate example of mitigated speech in his best-selling book, *Outliers.* He explains what occurred on a day that I, and many other Washingtonians, vividly remember. On January 13, 1982 a massive blizzard engulfed Washington, D.C., causing the government to shut down at 3:00 p.m. As a result, thousands of people attempted to simultaneously navigate the snow-packed streets. It resulted in a traffic jam that caused my normal 30-minute drive from the U.S. Capitol to my home in McLean, Virginia to last over six hours. But there were more significant problems than clogged streets and an arduous drive home. That afternoon, Air Florida Flight 90 crashed into the Potomac River at the very road I was attempting to drive over, the Fourteenth Street Bridge. All but four passengers and one flight attendant died in the crash.

Gladwell explains that part of the reason for the crash was mitigated speech between the first officer and the captain. In cultural deference to the captain, the first officer only made veiled suggestions about his belief that the ice building up on the wings made it unsafe to attempt a takeoff. His repeated suggestions, veiled as they were, went unheeded by the captain. The result was not only tragic, but also completely avoidable... if only the captain had heard and heeded the hidden counsel of his first officer.

[1] Frank Tyger
[2] P190, *To Sell is Human*
[3] Tom Paciorek American baseball player.
[4] Slattery, *Kill the Elevator Speech*, 2014, Page 10
[5] *Skill in Communication: A Vital Element in Effective Management*, By David D. Acker
[6] Maxwell, *Relationships* 101, 2003, Page 42
[7] McGee, *How to Succeed With People*, 2013, Page 160
[8] Thomas Friedman, Author
[9] *Power Questions*, Page 14
[10] Stephen R. Covey
[11] Covey, *The Speed of Trust*, 2006, Page 214
[12] Fox, *How to Become a Rainmaker*, 2000, Pages 80-82

Chapter 10
The Power of Smart Silence

Selling is not telling and *you can't listen when your mouth is moving.*[1]

In the previous chapter, we explored the four types of listening; Pseudo, Easy, Smart and Astute. We then explored two of six suggestions to assist you with the critical skill of astute listening:

1. Check your Mindset: Plan to Listen.

2. Turn on Your Sensors.

In this chapter, we'll explore the remaining four suggestions.

3. Remember the Power of Smart Silence

Business Analyst Peter Drucker said, "The most important thing in communication is hearing what isn't said." To hear what isn't being said, remember the interesting coincidence that *listen* and *silent* both have the same letters. You cannot do one without the other.

Veterans of selling know that silence sells. They understand Frank Tyger's insight, "You can only improve on saying nothing by saying nothing often."[2]

A good way to develop the mindset of smart silence is to understand how police and fire public safety radios work. To communicate with each other, their radios must be on the same frequency band. Additionally, they use what is known as a half-duplex system where each party must respect the other and be courteous. Like the Walkie-Talkies many of us had as kids, their radios have a button you must

Push-to-talk (PTT.) After speaking, you must release the button to listen. If both parties Push-to-talk at the same time there is no communication. (By the way, your phone is a full duplex system that allows two people to speak at the same time. Curiously, this capability often diminishes effective communication. Go figure.)

At your next meeting, I suggest you go in with a mindset of smart silence. Take a moment to get on the same frequency as those with whom you are speaking and avoid the urge to hit the Push-to-talk button. Don't talk over others, finish their sentences, interrupt, or begin to answer their questions before they finish asking them.

Instead, determine to let others hold the PTT button while you smartly listen, absorb, and process important information. Catch the:

- *Obvious, easy content*

- *Understatements*

- *Micro-comments*

- *Micro-disclosures*

- *Matters of major importance to your customer buried in seemingly off-handed statements*

> ## *You can't listen while you are talking*
> ## *Think of PTT – Push-to-talk!*

To learn more and hear what isn't being said, remember what your job is:

"Your job is not to listen and respond. Your job is to gain information and create a vibrant dialogue. That's an important distinction. TELL ME MORE is the magic key to open up the next layer of the person's thinking and experiences."[3]

4. Curb Your Enthusiasm to Talk

The brilliant consultant Dan Sullivan reminds his clients, "You cannot sell what John Smith buys until you see with John Smith's eyes."

Taking the time required to see with your customers' eyes is not easy.

Especially if you're genuinely eager to help them and confident that you have products to mitigate their pain and meet their needs. If your customers feel like you are trying to sell a product before understanding their needs and requirements, their guard goes up and trust goes down.

Avoid the urge to lead the customer to your answer or premature product push. It will build priceless trust and result in the customer having more faith in your judgment and more faith in your word.

Be mindful that no one likes to feel coerced.

"Unfortunately, many buyers feel that salespeople try to force or coerce a fit. No matter what you put in front of the word 'selling' (consultative, solution, visionary, creative, integrity, value-based), it's still tainted with the association of a person doing something to somebody, rather than *for* or *with* them. Even talented and ethical sales professionals can be **judged guilty until proven innocent of failing to** *listen*."[4]

Be intentional about maximizing your pre-RFP TIFOC (Time In Front Of Customer) by listening. Most sales people aren't good at this. According to Miller-Heiman, during an average hour spent with customers, the sales person speaks a whopping 48 minutes or 80% of the time.

To curb your enthusiasm to talk instead of listen, it helps to understand the permutations of speaking and listening:

- *The customer speaks, you don't listen.*
- *The customer speaks, you disagree.*
- *The customer speaks, you ignore.*
- *The customer speaks, you spin it and hear it differently (This is called happy ears or confirmation bias.)*
- *The customer speaks, you listen, but you don't act.*
- *The customer speaks, you listen, you respond, and you win!*

Curbing our enthusiasm to speak is difficult for another reason. As listeners, we can think faster than others can speak.

According to researchers at the University of Missouri, most of us speak at the rate of about 125 words per minute. However, we have the mental capacity to understand someone speaking at 400 words per minute. (So we have the capacity to listen three times faster than our customers talk.) This delta makes it very tempting for our minds to grow restless and wander... particularly if your brain has an exceptionally fast processor coupled with a personality disposition of impatience!

5. Know Your Goals

When with your customer, in addition to your typical meeting goals, I suggest that you establish your SLO (Single Listening Objective). This means going into each meeting with a predetermined mindset. To get you started, following are some checklist suggestions for you to consider.

Do Checklist

✓ Be intentional about what you want to do, ask, learn, observe, or avoid in your meetings with the customer.

✓ Do you want to probe?

✓ What do you want to discover?

✓ What biases or prejudices do you need to control?

✓ Is your goal to:

- Give insight or get insight?

- Impress the customer with your intellect or your interest?

- Impress the customer with your smart answers or your smart questions?

- Impress the customer with your learnedness or your listening?

✓ Is your goal to keep the customer conversation going so there is a reason and value for them to have another meeting?

✓ Is your goal to be referred to another customer to meet?

Don't Do Checklist

- ✗ Don't interrupt.

- ✗ Don't let your agenda and goals for the meeting trump the customer's goals. Their agenda beats yours.

- ✗ Don't be arrogant or a know-it-all.

- ✗ Don't pontificate.

- ✗ Don't forget to create a digital-free zone. (No looking at any of your electronic devices when with the customer.)

Let me add one final behavior to the avoid checklist. Don't play, *Name That Tune*. You might be familiar with this old parlor game. The goal of the game is to quickly identify a song that's being played. The person who can name the song with the fewest notes played is the winner.

When meeting with customers, it's tempting to play *Name That Tune*. After briefly listening to them we want to jump in and impress them with our lightning-fast comprehension and brilliant responses. Guess what? Customers do not want to play *Name That Tune*. They want to play their entire song. They want to finish speaking. They want to tell us their story without interruption. They want us to impress them with our listening.

So resist the urge to listen to a customer's initially stated problem and then jump in with a quick diagnosis. This is what Mike Bosworth calls premature solutioning. In medicine, it's called malpractice. Remember, "Some people need to tell you their story before they're ready to hear your solution."[5]

Let's use a military analogy. You can come in strong with Shock and Awe like a B-52 carpet bombing your customers with facts or an A-10 Warthog spraying words from a Gatling gun at them without you taking a breath.

Or you can come in quiet and low observable like the F-22 Stealth fighter listening with acute sensors. I think you would agree – bombarding your customer with words is a bad strategy that is too often employed.

6. Be a Hacker, Not a Yacker

Who do you know who needs a good listening to today?[6]

No one ever learned anything by yacking away. The goal is to *hack* into the minds of your customers without invading their privacy.

Take a lesson from the National Security Agency. Be a hacker. Like the NSA, learn to monitor, collect, sweep, synthesize, and understand the data your customer is sending you. Listen to them with so much respect, skill, and interest that you can hack into their soul and understand them more deeply than others do.

Remember, your customer is hoping you're skilled enough to capture those things that matter most to them. In this case, hacking is not illegal... it's brilliant!

Like a good intelligence officer, look for E.E.I. (Essential Elements of Information.) Look for Emotional State-of-Mind and Type of Communicator.

Emotional State-of-Mind

While appearing to be engaged in casual conversation, be quietly watching, listening, discerning, seeing, sensing:

- Are they angry or anxious?
- Are they getting ready to retire or move on to another assignment?
- Are their heads and hearts still engaged in their work?
- Can you detect the sotto voco? (The quiet comments densely packed with importance.)
- What is their state of mind?
- What are their visions, values, and vicissitudes?
- Who frustrated them in the past? How? Why?
- Who pleased them in the past? How? Why?
- What drives them, stresses them, ticks them off, or turns them on?
- What are their FUDs – Fears, Uncertainties, and Doubts?

Type of Communicator

- Are they internal processors or verbal processors?

- Do they make decisions: Fast/slow/not at all?

- Do they have big, strong, secure, or fragile egos?

- Where are they with their professional and personal levels of maturity, security, competence, etc.?

- What are their personality types?

In closing this section, remember that in the world of procurements, everyone agrees that listening to the customer is important. But embracing the power of listening and smart silence needs to move beyond an ostensible value. It needs to become a mindset that morphs into a skillset. This skill is more challenging than most people anticipate and more rewarding than they imagine. To keep you motivated to keep developing your listening ability, remember:

"Wisdom is the reward you get for a lifetime of listening when you'd have preferred to talk."[7]

"Courage is what it takes to stand up and speak; courage is also what it takes to sit down and listen."[8]

---

[1] David G. Pugh, Ph.D.
[2] D. Acker, *Skill in Communication: A Vital Element in Effective Management*
[3] Andrew Sobel, *Power Questions*, Page 85
[4] Khalsa and Illig, *Let's Get Real Or Let's Not Play*, 2008, Page 3
[5] McGee, *How to Succeed With People*, 2013, Page 160
[6] McGee, *How to Succeed With People*, 2013, Page 161
[7] Doug Larson
[8] Winston S. Churchill

Chapter 11
The Power of Smart Questions

Questions are the answer.[1]

Two Jesuit novices both wanted a cigarette while they prayed. They decided to ask their superior for permission. The first asked but was told no. A little while later, he spotted his friend smoking and praying. "Why did the superior allow you to smoke and not me?" he asked. His friend replied, "Because you asked if you could smoke while you prayed, and I asked if I could pray while I smoked!"

W. Edwards Deming, founder of the quality movement, said: *"If you do not know how to ask the right question, you discover nothing."*[2] In both our professional and personal lives, the art of asking the right questions is one of the most important skillsets we can learn. It is also the most easily overlooked. For many of us, the habit of asking smart questions is a forgotten skill.

The next time you observe your colleagues preparing for an important customer meeting, watch where they invest their time in preparation and planning. The chances are good that before the meeting you will see them scrambling to get good intel about the customer. You might see them prepare and practice comments about your company and the services it provides. If they're going to visit a DoD customer, there is a high probability they will be focused on building a PowerPoint presentation so they can more fully inform the customer about their enterprise and proposed solution.

There is one other high probability; they will invest almost no time thinking about smart, specific questions they intend to ask the customer. Like teaching cursive writing to third graders, the skillset of asking smart questions is a dying art. For all of us, it's a critical challenge to rediscover this Billion Dollar Mindset.

In this chapter, we'll look at the function of questions and the four categories of questions. But first, let's remind ourselves why the mindset of asking smart questions is critical to success.

- Albert Einstein once said that if he had an hour to solve a problem and his life depended on it, he would use the first 55 minutes to determine the proper questions to ask. He also said, "I have no special talents. I am only passionately curious."[3]

- After changing the world by developing the polio vaccine, Jonas Salk said this: "What people think of as the moment of discovery is really the discovery of the question."[4]

- "Insightful questions build credibility and deepen relationships."[5]

- "Telling creates resistance. ASKING CREATES RELATIONSHIPS."[6]

- "Open conversations [questions] generate loyalty, sales and most of all, learning... for both sides."[7]

According to DoD Source Selection Procedures, "Meaningful communications with Industry should begin early during the development of contract requirements and the acquisition strategy. To ensure the best possible proposals from Industry and the best possible outcome for the Government, the SST (Source Selection Team) should provide opportunities for meaningful interactions with Industry, including one-on-one meetings with individual firms."[8]

Notice in the above procedural recommendations that one word appears twice: the word *meaningful*. As an entity, the government understands the importance of *meaningful* moments with industry partners. When you get an appointment with the people within that entity, they are hoping that you have the skillsets necessary to create *meaningful* moments with them. They want you to know how to participate in a dialogue that enhances discovery, insight, and understanding. They want you to understand their presented problem. They want you to surprise them with your desire to grasp the deeper complexity of their challenges. And while doing this, they are also hoping you conduct yourself in such a way that time spent with you is valuable and maybe even enjoyable. When you do these things, there are two outcomes: 1) You find it much easier to get follow-up meetings with the customer and 2) You quickly differentiate yourself from your competitors.

How do you create meaningful dialogue? You begin by recapturing the mindset of asking astute questions. You determine to enter every customer engagement with a resolute focus on the power of questions. In every interaction, you make it your goal to ask questions that are genuine, pertinent, and appropriate. As Confucius said, "The man who asks a question is a fool for a minute, the man who does not ask is a fool for life." So, ask!

For some people, it's helpful to remember the Eagles song, *Busy Being Fabulous*. The song is a brilliant story of a woman who misses the satisfaction of great relationships with her family because she is *too busy being fabulous.* In the procurement world, many contractors never develop a deep understanding of their customer because they are too busy being fabulous. In their critical one-on-one meetings, instead of impressing the customer with smart questions, they try to impress the customer with how fabulous they, their company, or their products are. People who are busy being fabulous rarely create the desire in their customer to promptly schedule a follow-up meeting. Remember, your goal is not to get the first meeting with your customer. That is professional courtesy *from* your customer. Your goal is to get to the second, tenth, and twenty-fifth meeting with your customer.

Why Questions Matter

When preparing for any customer interaction, remember that the questions you ask are often far more powerful than any content or information you share. Smart questions enable you to get to the heart of your customers' problems or needs more accurately and quickly, without your customers feeling pushed.

Why are questions such a game-changer in customer interactions? Because smart questions enhance the quality of your meetings, engage your customers, and quietly nudge your relationship with your customers to the right on the Relationship Continuum. Additionally, when asked skillfully:

- *Questions are the discovery mechanism of understanding.*

- *Questions are a sign of respect for those you meet.*

- *Questions are proof of your interest in another person.*

- *Questions are a building block of trust.*

- *Questions are evidence of following the counsel of Stephen Covey, "Seek first to understand."*

- *Questions are what make time with you positively unique.*

When you begin a meeting with a mindset of asking questions, several immediate benefits kick in. Initially, they serve as your private memory jogger to, *focus on the customer and stop trying to be fabulous*! They also set the tone of the meeting, one where the customer immediately senses that you're there to interact with them rather than give a commercial to them.

Most importantly, when you start a meeting with smart questions, they enable you to begin the meeting with what I call *forced clarity*. Your questions direct your customer to tell you with great precision what would make their time with you most valuable to them. When you discover what they value, you can then instantly adapt your agenda to fit their highest priorities.

The Four Categories of Questions

In preparing a mindset of asking questions, there are four categories of questions to choose from: Rapport Questions, Orientation Questions, Smart Questions, and Relationship-Shifting Questions. Each category serves a specific purpose. Collectively, they are profoundly significant. Your challenge is to know how and when to use questions from each category.

1. Rapport Questions

Rapport questions are used to set the tone of a meeting. They are generally used at the outset of a meeting when people are still settling in and preparing to get into the more serious purpose of the meeting.

They are the small-talk questions that kick start an atmosphere of people feeling welcomed and recognized. They also set the stage for an atmosphere of professionally friendly interaction.

Rapport questions are as simple as:

Is this your first time here?

Did you have any trouble getting here?

How was traffic on your drive here?

Would you like a cup of coffee or some water before we begin?

If you've previously met the customer and have moved to the right on the Relationship Continuum, you can use questions that re-establish rapport. The questions can be a simple as:

It's nice to see you again. How have you been?

How is your day going?

Have you been up to anything interesting lately?

What's new in your world?

Depending on the importance of a meeting and its allotted time, rapport questions may last a few seconds or a few minutes. Unless you're in a very formal meeting, don't overlook the importance of these questions. While appearing innocuous, they subtly shape the atmosphere of your interaction.

Admittedly, you need to be aware that some people (including corporate leaders) completely miss the importance of these brief human moments. Some people avoid them because they are uncomfortable with small talk. These people immediately want to get into the reason we are here because they have no idea how to engage in this unstructured banter of one human being to another.

Others avoid rapport questions because of the urgency of the meeting and the press of limited time. This is absolutely valid. And still others avoid these questions because it's a power play to them. In their mind, they are so important and so busy they have transcended the need to be mindful of the human beings in their presence.

2. Orientation Questions

Orientation questions set the vector of your meeting. They give the meeting a focus and direction that aligns the meeting objectives with what is important to your customer. Consider some of these sample questions:

I want to be mindful of your schedule. We have 25 minutes scheduled for this meeting. Does that amount of time still work for you?

*What **one thing** would make this time most valuable to you?*

Of course I have some questions I'd like to ask and a couple of thoughts that I'd like to share. But more than that, I'd like to know from your perspective, what would make this meeting a good use of your time?

In our brief time together, if we could only discuss three items, what would you choose?

The original purpose of our meeting when we scheduled it was to discuss "X." Is that still okay with you or are there some other issues you'd prefer to discuss?

When you take the time to ask orientation questions, *pay attention to the answer*. Orientation questions require you to have the agility to instantly adapt your agenda to that of the customer. If you ask these questions but then default to your predetermined agenda, you lose creditability with your customer.

3. Smart Questions

Smart questions are those that get to the heart of the matter. They facilitate a deep understanding of your customer's program needs, challenges, and goals. They also help you understand your customer's pressures, priorities, and pain. Smart questions allow you to get into the world of your customer so that you can see what they see, hear what they want, and sense what they feel. Smart questions include:

What is the one thing you most wish we understood?

If we could change one thing, what would you want changed?

What is your operational pain?

What are your top three biggest challenges for this program?

What outcomes do you need or want?

What do you most want us to know, fix, or act upon?

Who are your end users and what do they want? What do they want more of? What do they want less of? What is making them crazy with frustration?

How can we help meet your mission?

Smart questions are even more important if you're serving a DoD customer. If that is not your world, I suggest you skip the next couple of paragraphs and go directly to the last category of questions. If it is, allow me to briefly get "into the weeds" of this world as we wander into the arcane language of contracting. (Fair warning, you are about to get brain freeze.)

An updated DoD Source Selection Procedures was published in April 2016. The biggest change is the VATEP (Value Adjusted Total Evaluated Price) tradeoff process. Per these procedures:

"When using this method, the SST [Source Selection Team] should ask the RO [Requirements Owner]: What is the Government willing to pay for higher quality performance between threshold (minimum) and objective (maximum) criteria? The solicitation specifies the value for each parameter that provides additional value to the Government." This means you need to understand even more about the requirements and which ones have more mission worth and value. The stronger your relationship, the more you can understand and gain insight into what they truly value.

To get this information, you need to ask some specific questions:

What are the most important requirements?

What are your stretch/objective requirements?

Which threshold requirements have value if we can exceed them (even if we can't make it all the way to the objective)?

How would you rank the operational value of the Top 3 requirements?

What do you see as future requirements in the next 5 years? How can we help you prepare for those requirements?

If we were to invest some of our discretionary resources, what should we focus on?

Particularly in this Smart Question area, make sure you use open-ended questions. Words used for open-ended questions include, "Tell me about..." "Describe..." and "How did this happen?" As David Acker says, "If you wish to explore a subject in more detail, avoid questions beginning with Do, Is and Are. They can be answered with one word."[9]

4. Relationship-Shifting Questions

Relationship-shifting questions are both the most powerful and the most overlooked of the four question categories. When used correctly, they are transformative in their power. They can effortlessly move your relationship with your customer off the left edge of the Relationship Continuum.

Relationship-shifting questions bring moments of humanity into your conversations. They are brief interchanges that fill a room with unexpected microbursts of laughter, fun discovery, fascinating connections, or rich candor. Create moments like these with your customer and you will find that they begin to welcome future meetings with you.

At their core, relationship-shifting questions are those that demonstrate your genuine interest in your customer. They are questions of sincerity and curiosity about your customer that are slightly outside the scope of your normal business talking points. They are simple questions like:

I'm always fascinated to learn of someone's journey, so how did you come to be doing what you do?

We'll get started in ninety seconds, but I was curious, what do you enjoy doing when you are not working?

As we get ready to roll into the weekend, are you doing anything fun or exciting this weekend?

What was your favorite assignment when you were in the military?

How did you become so skilled at what you do?

When you take time to practice a mindset of asking sincere,

relationship-shifting questions, you give someone a gift of your time and your interest. You give them a microburst of feeling important and valued as a human being. In short, you're putting the spotlight of attention on them. When you do this, you create a moment with them that is different than almost every other exchange they will have that day. In the process, you differentiate yourself from the competition.

Some Cautions about Questions

I hope you will begin to dust off the habit of asking smart questions. I highly recommend that you rediscover the life-changing mindset of asking questions. But while doing so, remember three things:

1. Don't go overboard asking too many questions. Don't make your customer feel like you're a CIA agent drilling them for information under a hot interrogation light. Remember the advice of Zig Ziglar, "Socratic questioning is often used by attorneys to get a witness to reveal a piece of information in court. The problem is that buyers should not be "tested" like witnesses on the witness stand."[10]

2. The timing of your questions must be appropriate. Deciding that you want to practice the skill of asking questions does not mean you suddenly have carte blanche to ask anyone any question at any time. Wisdom is needed in the judicious use of this skill.

3. Pay attention to the tone of your voice when you ask questions. When you ask questions with a tone of voice filled with curiosity and genuine interest, others rarely find your questions off-putting. I understand that some experts tell you to never begin questions with "why." Others tell you to never begin questions with "how." I understand the psychology and reasoning of both of these positions. In practice, when you learn to speak with a tone of voice that makes people feel safe, they are usually open to your question regardless of the opening word.

How Questions Work in Real Life

Recently, my wife and I had dinner with a couple that we hadn't seen in a year. Michael and Marcia are two of those special people that are a pleasure to be with. Dinner with them is guaranteed to be filled with fun, laughter, and great conversation. This night was no exception.

As we caught up with each other's lives, we asked if they'd been up to anything unique or interesting. Michael chuckled and mentioned that they were spending most of their free time away from home. He then explained, "Our kids are in their mid-twenties now, and they love spending time with their friends at the lake. It occurred to us that if we want extended time with our kids, we need to go where they are... because they sure aren't wanting to hang around the house with us!"

Then he explained how they went to a marina to look at some pontoon boats. When they walked into the marina, the sales person introduced himself and asked if he could help them. They explained that they wanted to look at pontoon boats. Rather than walking them directly to that part of the marina, the salesperson suggested they sit down and chat. He then proceeded to bring them some coffee and ask them some questions. Sincere questions. Smart questions. He asked them why they wanted a pontoon boat. How would they use it? How many people would be on it? What about boating or being on the water interested them? Where do they sleep when they go to the lake? For well over an hour, this individual just asked questions, listened carefully, and took notes about what they wanted. He realized they were not looking for a specific product. Rather, they were looking for a specific experience that they hoped the right product would provide.

That day, when Michael and Marcia left the marina, they didn't walk out as owners of a pontoon boat. They left as owners of a fully equipped 38-foot speedboat. Three months later, they returned that boat to purchase a 48-foot yacht that allows them to travel up and down the waterways of America for weeks at a time.

What happened over that unhurried cup of coffee? Did a slick salesman manipulate my friends into an impetuous decision? On the contrary, they were not hustled, they were understood. The salesman took the time to understand their primary desires and their end goals. And then he showed them how these could be more fully satisfied with another kind of watercraft. They hadn't met a shyster; they met someone with a mindset of astute listening while asking smart questions.

That is the power of smart questions. Questions help you understand your customer and enable you to meet their needs, solve their problems, and provide custom fit solutions that were not even on the radar screen of their mind's eye. Remember, stop being *busy being fabulous* and get busy developing a mindset of asking smart questions.

---

[1] Zig Ziglar
[2] http://www.brainyquote.com/quotes/quotes/w/wedwardsd384036.html
[3] http://amorebeautifulquestion.com/einstein-questioning/
[4] http://www.azquotes.com/quote/557996
[5] Jill Konrath (expert Sales Consultant)
[6] Andrew Sobel, *Client Relationships* and author of *Power Questions*
[7] Seth Godin [http://sethgodin.typepad.com/seths_blog/2011/10/open-conversations-or-close-them.html]
[8] Claire M. Grady, Director, Defense Procurement and Acquisition Policy, *DoD Source Selection Procedures*, 4/1/2016
[9] David D. Acker, *Skill in Communication: A Vital Element in Effective Management*
[10] Ziglar, *Zig Ziglar's Secrets of Closing the Sale*, 1984, Page 34

Part Four:
The Power of
Smart Trust

Chapter 12
Why Trust Matters

More and more CEOs have become conscious that they are the CEO of marketing. You're selling trust.[1]

If customer relationships had a Periodic table like chemistry, the three primary elements with the highest atomic numbers would be listening, trust and likeability. In this chapter we want to examine the element of trust.

Why Does Trust Matter?

The inimitable Zig Ziglar said there are five reasons for a buyer *not* to buy. They are: no need, no money, no desire, no urgency, and no trust. Notice the final reason he listed: trust. Zig recognized, "If people like you, they'll listen to you, but if they trust you, they'll do business with you."

How important is trust? Trust is the most important thing you build. Not systems, not products, not services… but trust. Trust is the *sine quo non* (from Latin, meaning "without which nothing") of successful business relationships. It's the currency of interaction and agreements, the link between getting to know a customer and getting business with a customer. It's the dealmaker and the tiebreaker.

People do business with people they like and trust – period. As John Maxwell puts it, "All things being equal, people will work with people they like; all things not being equal, they still will."[2]

Ceteris paribus is a Latin phrase meaning "other things being equal or held constant." Government procurement tries to technically level bidders, but they can't level relationship or trust. In the final analysis, trust is the difference maker. And those who demonstrate trust with the same passion with which they deliver great products are those who win, keep, and grow business.

Trust directly impacts business results. In, *The Speed of Trust*, Stephen Covey develops an insightful formula to show how trust directly impacts two outcomes – the speed of business and the cost of business. Specifically:

> "When trust goes down, speed will also go down and costs will go up.
>
> **Trust** ↓ = **Speed** ↓ **Cost** ↑
>
> When trust goes up, speed will also go up and costs will go down.
>
> **Trust** ↑ = **Speed** ↑ **Cost** ↓
>
> It's that simple, that real, and that predictable."[3]

The impact of trust on the speed of business has been demonstrated in the aerospace and defense industries. The Lockheed Skunkworks, led by Kelly Johnson, was famous for leveraging trust to accomplish amazing feats. The U-2 spy airplane was built in 90 days. Other Herculean and rapid efforts included the SR-71 Blackbird and the F-117 Nighthawk stealth fighter. The maiden flight of the Nighthawk took place in 1981 and the aircraft miraculously achieved initial operating capability status in 1983. Some examples of trust statements from Kelly Johnson's famous 14 Skunkworks principles include:

#12) "There must be absolute trust between the military project organization and the contractor with very close cooperation and liaison on a day-to-day basis. This cuts down misunderstanding and correspondence to an absolute minimum.

#6) Don't have the books ninety days late and don't surprise the customer with sudden overruns."

Kelly Johnson understood that, "When people trust each other, they stop playing games, they look beyond temporary problems, and they expose themselves with less hesitation."[4]

Keys to Building Trust

"According to a study conducted by the New York Sales and Marketing Club, 71% of the people who buy from you do so because they like you, trust you, and respect you. The **word *trust* includes 'us'.** A bond must be formed between you and the prospect before anything significant will be bought or sold."[5]

Here are some simple behaviors to bolster trust:

- Communicate openly. (They can see through you if you are not transparent.)

- Be believable. "Always be truth-telling. A half-truth is a whole lie."[6]

- Deliver what you promise.

- Make trust deposits. Mike Abrashoff, states, "Trust is like a bank account – you have got to keep making deposits if you want it to grow. On occasion, things will go wrong, and you will have to make a withdrawal. Meanwhile, it's sitting in the bank earning interest."[7]

- Keep commitments. Stephen Covey concludes that trust is the one thing that can build or destroy every human relationship. Keeping commitments is what Covey refers to as the "Big Kahuna" of all the trust behaviors. Covey further states: "Trust builds longevity of relationships. A low trust organization will have to constantly find new customers." He sums up with, "Trust equals confidence and distrust equals suspicion."

- Offer unvarnished truth. Regarding the importance of trust, Salzberg observes:

"Trust is like oxygen for a business. When it's in short supply, the effect for employees and customers alike can be like a loss of cabin pressure on an aircraft. And never has the danger been higher than it is now in the viral conditions of the Twitter Age.

"Against these seemingly unstoppable high-tech forces, I am heartened that even today, trust and transparency still can emanate from the ultimate in low-tech: a leader standing flat-footed in a room, listening and offering, as best he or she can, the plain, unvarnished truth."[9]

- Pass the test drive. Your customers test-drive your trust on every action item. If you can't get the little things right, your customers won't trust you on the big things.

"People trust what they see over what they hear. Trust is simply whether the customer believed you. Help customers see what they can't. Trust is a peculiar resource; it's built rather than depleted by use."[8]

"Trust, but verify" was a line Ronald Reagan made famous in his dealings with the former Soviet Union. But real trust means you don't have to verify; trust with verification is not actually trust.

- Find a model blueprint for contractor behavior. Picture an honest small town carpenter, like someone from Mayberry, on the Andy Griffith Show. Why do you trust them?

Because:

1. *They don't do work that doesn't need to be done.*

2. *They refer you to another specialist (e.g. plumber, electrician, etc.) if the task is beyond their expertise or scope.*

3. *They offer a creative solution to save money. They provide value.*

4. *They offer options and tradeoffs without pushing or forcing a solution.*

5. *They display consistent behavior.*

Choose Your Camp

A friend of mine regularly encourages his team to choose how they want to be viewed by their customers. To clarify their thinking, he contrasts two fictitious characters: Good-Guy and Dr. Evil.

Good-Guy is a trusted advisor. Dr. Evil lacks the trust to build strong relationships. He suggests that his team consider what customers say to themselves after meeting with each of them.

Good-Guy – Trusted Advisor

"It's great to work with Good-Guy. A friend that vouched for his character and expertise referred him to me. He's open and transparent. He listens well. He doesn't hide problems, he discloses them. He cares about me. He is not self-focused. His word is gospel. When he makes a promise or commitment, I can count on it. He always surpasses his commitments and provides more value. He always takes copious notes. He listens carefully and pays attention to details that matter to me. It's good having an ally on the same page. He's a straight shooter. If he messes up, he apologizes, takes responsibility, and recovers fast. He's a professional friend."

Dr. Evil – Lacks Trust

"I get an uneasy feeling after meeting with Dr. Evil. He's so focused on himself; I don't think I trust him. He may go around my back to my boss or Congress if he doesn't get what he wants. He's always talking about how much commission he'll make on our deal. He expects me to buy at our first meeting. I don't even know him. I wish he took some notes. In larger meetings, he's always preoccupied and often has his head down and eyes closed like he's praying. Actually, he's just texting under the table. He rarely follows up with the meeting actions unless I ping him to remind him. Why is it my responsibility to manage the commitments he made to me?"

All of us need a mindset that remembers the power of trusted relationships. "Without customers' trust, the rest doesn't matter."[9]

In the end, trust builds delighted customers. Customers who feel *glad* without ever feeling *had.*

---

[1] Phillip Kotler
[2] Maxwell, Team. 2004, Page 517
[3] Covey, *The Speed of Trust*, 2006, Page 13
[4] Kawasaki, *Enchantment*, 2011, Page 28
[5] Ziglar, *Zig Ziglar's Secrets of Closing the Sale*, 1984, Page 34
[6] Yiddish Proverb
[7] Maxwell, Team. 2004, Page 405
[8] Bradberry and Greaves, *Emotional Intelligence 2.0*, 2009, Page 186 & 191
[9] Covey, *The Speed of Trust*, 2006, Page 271

Chapter 13
Trust Equations

*Hype is the ultimate oversell. The worst thing about hype is that by
definition it's impossible to fulfill its promise.[1]*

*It must be amusing to be in the heating and air-conditioning business.
With perfect predictability, the first hot day of summer brings frantic
calls from people who discover that their air-conditioning system is
broken. This happened to my neighbors.*

*Don and Paula went away for several days. They returned to the
unhappy discovery of walking into a home that was a sauna-soothing
ninety-three degrees. They quickly called three companies to come
and give them a repair estimate. They hoped the repair would be
quick, easy and inexpensive. However, not wanting to be blindsided,
they also planned for the news that they might need to replace their
twelve-year-old unit and estimated the cost could be as much as
$8,000.*

*The first company to respond gave them the news that their system
was on life support. They could patch it back together for a few
hundred bucks or they could bite the bullet and replace the entire
system... for twice their worst estimate. After meeting with the
company spokesperson, they did something amazing. They called the
other two contractors and told them not to come to their home. Then
they agreed to have a $16,000 air-conditioning system installed by a
company they had never done business with.*

*When I asked them why they had made such a seemingly hasty
decision, their answer was telling. They replied: "The spokesperson
for the company reeked of integrity. We trusted him and his*

> *recommendations." They have never regretted their decision.*
>
> *It doesn't matter if a customer is buying a $16,000 air-conditioning unit for their home or a $116,000,000 piece of electronic equipment for an aircraft carrier, trust is profoundly determinative of who we choose to do business with.*

Stephen Covey is correct when he states that: "Trust is the glue of life. It's the most essential ingredient in effective communication. It's the foundational principle that holds all relationships."[2]

And it is a vital element in winning and keeping business.

What is Trust?

"Trust is a function of character and competence. Character includes your integrity, your motive, and your intent with people (like self-orientation below.) Competence includes your capabilities, your skills, your results, and your track record. And both are vital."[3]

Some trust is based on brand, and your company's brand will qualify you for the opportunity. But since agencies buy from people, it's your *personal* brand that wins the day. Most trust is established through the people on the team, so ensure you have good people on your team and keep them committed to establishing trust with customers.

When we try to persuade customers to take action before trust is established, we realize customers are skeptics. They need to see more than a solo BD person as the face of the company.

Customers think to themselves,

Never have I:

- Met your Program Manager...
- Met your engineers...
- Met your leadership...
- Met your employees...
- Or even shared a coffee or a meal...

So, why should I do business with you?

To take the guesswork out of trust, it's useful to look at some trust equations that bring the quantitative aspects of this vital element into smart customer relationships.

Here is a popular equation for trust:

$$\textbf{Trust} = \{\textbf{Rapport x Credibility}\} / \textbf{Risk}^4$$

Another variant of the trust equation is:

$$\textbf{Trust} = \{\textbf{Credibility} + \textbf{Reliability} + \textbf{Intimacy}\} / \textbf{Self-Orientation}^5$$

Note: lowering your self-orientation increases trust.

Intuitively, both equations are correct. So let's combine the equations to develop just one. Also, to avoid improper overtones, the word "intimacy" may better be replaced with "rapport" for government contracting.

$$\textbf{Trust} = \{\textbf{Credibility} + \textbf{Reliability} + \textbf{Rapport}\} / \{\textbf{Risk} + \textbf{Self-Orientation}\}$$

To increase trust, we strive for ways to maximize the terms in the numerator and minimize the terms in the denominator.

To build-up trust, let's look at how to maximize each of these three terms in the numerator.

Credibility

To position with the customer, build credibility, acceptability.

To enhance your credibility, you must have:

- The right knowledge, expertise, and insights in this field.
- Experience and strong past performance. Show proof in CPARs (Contractor Performance Assessment Reports.) Performance is always your best salesperson.
- Case studies and demonstrated social proof through repeat business.
- References and powerful testimonials.

According to the Edelman Trust Barometer, only 8% of people trust what companies say about themselves. As such, it is a required strategy to get CPARs when you're performing well and/or a competitor is doing poorly. Typically, CPARs are intended to be issued yearly, but they often get delayed. Use your positive relationship to remind your government PM/PCO to complete your CPARs (if they are strong.) You must establish credibility and continually re-establish credibility. James Leggett points out that reputation is made in a moment, whereas character is built in a lifetime.

Remember, customers are assessing your competence, integrity, and character. In building trust and credibility, words matter, but character matters most.

When the government is evaluating who should receive a contract award, remember that they are trying to decide "Who do we want to walk into the future with us?" It's a big decision with long-term consequences.

Also, be aware that many sections of proposals are subjective, not fact-based multiple-choice questions. As such, if you have a pre-existing customer relationship where you are trusted and your credibility is known, these intangibles predispose the customer to give you a more positive subjective score. And, if you have some proposal weaknesses, you will often get the carry-over benefit of the doubt. (Similar to a credible long-time "A" student who slips a little but is given the benefit of the doubt.) Or they will ask you a question (in the form of an EN – Evaluation Notice) to help you shore up your position.

Reliability

> *Making commitments generates hope. Keeping commitments generates trust.*[6]

One of the easiest ways to understand the power of reliability is to consider the four possible options you have in combining *say* and *do*. "As you consider each option, keep in mind that say is declaring intent; do is carrying it out. Say is words; do is actions. Say is talk; do is walk. Say is promise; do is deliver."[7]

At the end of the day, our words are empty unless we follow them with the promised action.

Trust is built when our deeds match our words. Consider the USAA insurance company. They automatically sent 15,000 rebate checks on car insurance when soldiers were deployed. This created a huge trust score. Some soldiers returned the rebate saying they had been back on leave or someone else in the family used the car.

Do what you say you will do. Period.

In his blog, Seth Godin asks: "Where does trust come from?"

"Hint: it never comes from the good times and from the easy projects. We trust people because they showed up when it wasn't convenient, because they told the truth when it was easier to lie, and because they kept a promise when they could have gotten away with breaking it. Every tough time and every pressured project is another opportunity to earn the trust of someone you care about.

"In establishing a new relationship where you want to build trust fast, follow this process: Find a value-added reason to make a commitment and keep it... and do it again... and again... and again. As you implement this 'Make-Keep-Repeat' cycle, notice how quickly the Trust Account grows."[8]

Don't promise what you can't deliver.

It's not what you say, it's what you do.

"When selling our ideas, we tend to overpromise in our enthusiasm for our creation. In our vision of how we *hope* it will be, we leave no room for failure. The result will probably be disappointing – not disastrous, but a little less than expected. No one will say anything, they just won't trust you quite as much next time.

"Perhaps the most common broken promise of all is the one that is made with the intention – or at least the *hope* that it will be fulfilled. We call these 'best-case scenario (BCS) promises.' Promises such as these are likely to be kept, provided all the planets fall into perfect alignment. In other words, best-case scenario promises are *likely to be broken.* Companies need to learn how to avoid making best-case scenario promises."[9]

Over statements reduce trust. So in making promises, beware of what Tom Cargill, of Bell Labs cited as the *Ninety-Ninety Rule of Schedules for Software Coding*: The first 90% of the task takes 90% of the time, and the last 10% takes the other 90 %!

Let's face it, most customers are skeptics; they have been victims of over-promising and under-delivering. In government contracting, it's often a cost-plus contract for development. Therefore, broken promises translate into delays and cost growth. Rosy projections become troubled programs. Customer dissatisfaction grows when there is a significant difference between what they expected and what they got.

In politics, if you don't keep your promises to your constituents, you won't be re-elected. In business, if you don't keep your promises to your customers, you won't get a follow-on contract. There are polls to determine a political candidate's honesty and trustworthiness. If they polled you and your colleagues' honesty and trustworthiness, would you score high?

Revisiting the Trust Equation:

Trust={Credibility+Reliability+Rapport}/{Risk+Self-Orientation}

To build-up trust, minimize each of the two terms in the denominator: Risk and Self-Orientation.

Risk

"Assess risk from the government's point of view and your company's point of view."[10]

"And then there's risk. Customers always perceive risk. Will I waste money? Will I waste time? Can the contractor really do what they claim? Are they too small to deliver? Are they too large to care about our business? Is their technology too old? Is their approach too new?"[11]

A proposal is a pledge that you will deliver outcomes at specific points in the future. Many evaluators can be leery of over-promising and under-delivering. They worry about your ability to fulfill your proposed claims.

"Understanding that risk aversion is at the heart of the solutions sales process is crucial. It's why building a customer relationship is so important, why penetrating the federal market requires a major investment, and why the insiders get bigger and bigger. It isn't that federal officials don't want new contractors; it's that *they just want to sleep well at night*."[12]

There are three types of risk: process, performance, and personal.

"In customer relationships personal risk matters most and means: The decision-maker is fired or shuffled off to a lesser position in the organization. Realize that a bad selection decision affects the careers and personal lives of the deciders." [13]

Self-Orientation

The singer Toby Keith has a tongue-in-cheek song titled, *I Wanna Talk About Me.* The song is a light-hearted shot at individuals who relentlessly talk about themselves while never listening to others. One of the lyrics is: "I like talking about you, you, you, you… usually, but occasionally… I want to talk about me."

When it comes to your customer, resist the urge to talk about yourself and instead remember that your customer values time that is about them: Their world. Their priorities. Their concerns. Their expectations.

Develop a mindset to:

- Think like a customer. "Review what you're doing from your prospect's perspective."[14]

- Remember, some customers think, "It's bigger than you and me… It's all about me."[15]

- Remain resolute to focus on your customer: "Because it's not about you, it's about them."[16]

- Understand: "If you want to succeed with others, focus on meeting their needs first rather than your own. Perhaps your relationship with someone has stalled because you've not taken time to consider what they see as important and what they would value."[17]

Finally, "You can't give with strings attached – that is self-oriented."[18]

[1] Burg and Mann, *Go-Givers Sell More*, 2010, Page 136
[2] http://www.brainyquote.com/quotes/quotes/s/stephencov450798.html
[3] Covey, 2006
[4] Sources: Hy Silver & Tim Whalen
[5] Maister, 2000
[6] Blaine Lee
[7] Covey and Link, *Smart Trust*, 2012, Page 181
[8] Covey, *The Speed of Trust*, 2006, Page 220
[9] Denove and Power IV, *Satisfaction*, 2006, Page 105
[10] Robert Lohfeld, Lohfeld Consulting Group
[11] Sant, 2012
[12] White, *Rolling the Dice in DC*, 2006, Page 63
[13] Thull, 2003
[14] Jill Konrath
[15] Stephen Colbert
[16] Mark Rodgers
[17] McGee, *How to Succeed with People*, 2013, Page 111
[18] Robert Cialdini

Chapter 14
Tips to Build Trust

Bottom line: trust building is relationship building. If you don't build trust, you don't build relationships. No trust – no relationship; limited trust – limited relationship; strong trust – strong relationship.[1]

Trust is the invisible element with palpable power. For trust to become one of your distinguishing assets, it's necessary to recall how it's established, protected and practiced. In this chapter, we will briefly review this skill and the insights of other industry experts.

Rapport

The government can attempt to commoditize products and services, but it cannot commoditize relationships. This is the place where you have a huge opportunity to stand out. That begins by remembering that rapport is the seedbed of trust.

Let's look at some definitions of rapport. While reading them, ask yourself if these foundational habits are still part of your daily repertoire of customer engagement. (Remember, the challenge of smart customer relationships is rarely comprehension, it is application.)

"Rapport refers to a feeling of connection, trust, and understanding based on similar interests or character. When you have rapport with someone, there is a harmonious, mutual understanding that develops. The word rapport comes from a French phrase (and originally from Latin) meaning 'to bring back.' This is an interesting origin, and it hints at the idea of recalling shared interests, experiences, and memories ('Oh, I grew up in New York also!') Rapport begins to form when you identify things that you have in common with others, and engage in discussion about each other's interests and experiences."[2]

"A great conversation is one in which you find points of common interest, gracefully forge a bond through those interests, and allow the other person to shine. There is a word for that strong sense of harmonious accord: rapport."[3]

"According to the Encarta World English Dictionary, rapport is 'an emotional bond or friendly relationship between people based on mutual liking, trust, and a sense that they understand and share each other's concerns.'"[4]

"If you establish common ground with the other person, they will like you, believe you, begin to trust you, and connect with you on a deeper level. A 'things-in-common' level. The best way to win the connection is to first win the person."[5]

To win the person and build rapport:

- *"Commiserate.* Misery loves company. If the client wants to complain about anything from business to personal life, be a good supportive ear. You'll escalate the bonding process.

- *Be empathetic and care about them.* Be more interested in them than anyone else has ever been. There's a saying "If you want to be interesting, be interested. If you want to be fascinating, be fascinated."

- *Find the common ground.* One contractor had a difficult time bonding with a customer until they discovered they both liked the same band. In fact, they grew up listening to the same album. It was like a magic key to unlocking a bond that they shared. Find the common ground. Hunt for the things that you can relate to.

- *Mirror.* If you match your body language and tonality to what your prospects are doing and sounding like, they'll make the subconscious connection that you are like them. For example, if the customer leans forward, you lean forward. If the client tilts her head slightly, you can tilt yours the same way."[6]

If you saw the movie *Meet the Parents*, you undoubtedly remember the father-in-law, a former CIA agent, bringing his new son-in-law into the family *Circle of Trust*. The son-in-law had to earn the right to get into the circle of trust and then learn how to avoid being thrown out of it. The movie is a delightful comedy and a great analogy for those serving the government. Your goal is to be admitted into the customer's circle of trust and then remain there.

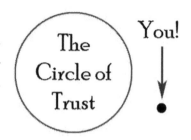

The Circle of Trust

To get into the circle of trust and remain there, remember these four tips:

Tip 1: Be a Trusted Advisor

Govies – nickname for government employees, are looking for an advisor, a confidant, and most of all an honest friend that will do business with their best interest at heart.

Carl Dickson at CapturePlanning.com writes:

"We all desperately want the kind of customer relationships where they call on us for advice and where we work together to solve problems as if we were one and the same organization. What a precious but rare thing that is. It doesn't happen like magic in a storybook. It happens because:

- *You were there for them when they needed it.*

- *You did things for them they couldn't do themselves.*

- *You solved problems they didn't even know they had before they even realized it.*

- *You made their jobs easier and were never a burden.*

- *You were easier to work with than their own staff.*

- *You were credible and they trusted you.*

- *You were available and they came to depend on you.*

- *You delivered insights and informed and taught them.*

Perhaps it's such a rare commodity because most contractors aspire to be like this but rarely are.

To become a trusted advisor, you have to put yourself in the frame of mind where you view your offerings from the customer's perspective –

what's in it for them. Then, you provide the advice – even if it doesn't include buying from your company! You're not there to sell; you're there to solve problems. The government universally despises salespeople, so your goal is not to sell yourself and your company; your goal is to become their trusted advisor."[7]

Tip 2: Be Transparent

The true meaning of trust requires being open and being transparent. If you're hiding something and the other person finds out, you will destroy trust. When you are open you will build trust.

Tip 3: Be Truthful (even when it hurts)

The only thing I know that is more exhausting than managing a program is trying to manage a lie. Reporting good news is easy. Reporting bad news is necessary.

"*Admit when you are wrong and apologize.* Sooner or later, you're going to screw up and let someone down. Things like failing to keep a commitment, having to go back on a promise, or missing a meeting or scheduled call shouldn't happen, but they sometimes do. When you make a mistake, face up to the situation as quickly as possible and apologize. Apologies and admitting where you have been wrong provides others with the opportunity to observe your character. Sincere apologies are accepted and appreciated, and they demonstrate your integrity (provided you are not apologizing for the same mistake again and again.)"[8]

Customers love contractors who have never burned them – ones that never did them wrong. But when you have an issue, socialize it; get on a customer roadshow, be the one to share to avoid surprises. When you self-report an issue you build trust. But when you try to hide an issue and the customer finds out through other channels, then you have violated trust. Trust is a slippery slope and it's a very steep climb back to the top to regain trust.

"Create transparency. Tell the truth in a way people can verify. Get real and genuine. Be open and authentic. Err on the side of disclosure. Operate on the premise of 'What you see is what you get.' Don't have hidden agendas. Don't hide information."[9]

Paradoxically, there is an upside to sharing bad news. As best-selling author Guy Kawasaki says, "When people see that they can believe you about bad stuff, they are more willing to believe you about good stuff."[10]

Unlike fine wine, bad news doesn't get better with time. So be pre-emptive, keep your customer community informed and messaged. Recall that, *disclosures of the truth precludes discovery of a white lie.*

Tip 4: Be Vulnerable

Self-disclosing, apologizing, and being human comes down to showing a little vulnerability.

"In the business world, however, vulnerability is often mistaken for weakness. Salespeople have traditionally been trained to have all the answers, to be superhuman, to be perfect. But it's hard to connect with perfection. As buyers, our BS meters go off. We know nobody's perfect; we know nobody has all the answers."[9]

Let go of the need to be perfect and the one with all the answers. It's okay not to know everything.

In one meeting, a GS civilian asked the business development guy a detailed technical question. Fortunately, he was smart enough to "phone a friend," and the chief engineer he called gave a strong answer. Saying I don't know but will get back to you ASAP is sometimes a powerful response. Embrace humility and have the courage to say you don't know. *Don't bluff – Get the answer.*

When you are truly competent, the customer likes when you are less than perfect. This vulnerability is illustrated in the political world.

"When the average candidate was clumsy, audiences liked him even less. But when the expert was clumsy, audiences liked him even more. Psychologists call this the pratfall effect. Spilling a cup of coffee hurt the image of the average candidate: it was just another reason for the audience to dislike him but the same blunder helped the expert appear human and approachable instead of superior and distant."[11]

Trust Builders

1. Build rapport, find common ground.

2. Avoid self-orientation, be about them not you.

3. Be transparent, disclose the truth.

4. Meet your commitments. Recover fast without excuses.

5. Be human. Be vulnerable. Admit when you're wrong and say you're sorry.

I know the name of the game is sales, but if you press or coerce the prospect to the degree that he senses that your life depends on that particular sale, he might wonder if it's his interest you have in mind or your own.

Trust Busters

1. Don't keep parachuting in different people – trust builds from person to person.

2. Don't be arrogant. Watch out for technical arrogance. Are your engineers legends in their own minds? Do your engineers spar with their counterparts? Do they lecture and pontificate? Do they talk at or with their counterparts? Buyers are buying your people and your engineers, and they have to work with them for years.

3. Don't use timid words that reduce trust or offer shallow promises. Using these phrases may backfire on building trust:

   Might – Hope to – Could – Possibly – To be honest with you – To tell you the truth – Honestly – Frankly – Truthfully – Trust me on this – Truth be told

"'Believe me... Trust me... Take it from me... If you want my opinion...' If you notice these phrases appearing in your language, we recommend you ferret them out and eliminate them. None of them is effective at conveying genuine value. They are all me-focused."[12]

If we build trust, foster open communications and collaboration across the government and industry, there is nothing we can't accomplish together – nothing!

If they don't like or trust you, they will find a way not to pick you. Get in the inner circle.

Persuasive honesty and a helping attitude are a combination your high-pressured competition might find hard to beat.

"Immediate and complete disclosure of your interests is a key component of trustworthiness. People will always wonder what your motivation is, so you should get this out of the way. Most people won't care that you are an interested or conflicted party as long as you disclose the relationship."[13]

Let the information above drive you to: "Clarify expectations. Disclose and reveal expectations. Discuss them. Validate them. Renegotiate them if needed and possible. Don't violate expectations. Don't assume that expectations are clear or shared."[14]

To gauge how well you are building customer trust, take the quiz below and then rate your score.

---

10 Question Scorecard

1. *Does your customer call you or is it always you calling them?*

2. *Does your customer call you outside work hours or on the weekend for advice?*

3. *Do reference customers call your customer without your begging? Are they promoters on your behalf? Will your customer refer you to other prospective customers?*

4. *Will you be notified of an RFI, Draft RFP or RFP release... or will you be surprised?*

5. *Do your executives show up and demonstrate their commitment? Do customers have their cell phone numbers?*

6. *Does your customer visit your company?*

7. *Does your customer willingly complete past performance questionnaires on your behalf without you hounding them?*

---

8. *Does your customer ask your advice about tradeoffs or choices?*

9. *Does your customer ask you for your future vision to help them with the art of the possible?*

10. *Does the customer ask for insight into their mission and requirements?*

Out of the 10 questions, how many did you answer "yes?" If you're like most of us, you could use more "yeses." Here are some benchmarks to self-assess your score.

7-10	Trusted Advisor
5, 6	Collaborative Industry Partner
3,4	Value-added Contractor
0-2	Transactional Vendor

Mindset Tips:

✓ People buy from people they like and trust, so become a trusted advisor. Empathize like a doctor or a nurse. Don't be like some politicians or used car salesperson.

✓ Live the equation:

Trust = {Credibility + Reliability + Rapport} / {Risk + Self-Orientation}

✓ If they don't like or trust you, they will always find a way not to pick you. If they *do* want you, you will usually get the contract (unless you mess up the proposal of course.)

[1] https://www.psychologytoday.com/blog/trust-the-new-workplace-currency/201309/ten-ways-cultivate-work-relationships-and-grow-trust
[2] Sobel, *All for One*, 2009, Page 88
[3] Burg and Mann, *Go-Givers Sell More*, 2010, Page 56
[4] Holmes, *The Ultimate Sales Machine*, 2007, Page 195
[5] Gitomer, *Little Black Book of Connections*, 2006, Page 157
[6] Holmes, *The Ultimate Sales Machine*, 2007, Page 197
[7] Carl Dickson
[8] Blount, *People Buy You*, 2010, Page 140-141
[9] Covey, *The Speed of Trust*, 2006, Page 157
[10] Guy Kawasaki, *The Art of the Start 2.0: The Time-Tested, Battle-Hardened Guide for Anyone*
[11] Grant, *Give and Take*, 2013, Page 134
[12] Burg and Mann, *Go-Givers Sell More*, 2010, Page 135
[13] Kawasaki, Enchantment, 2011, Page 30
[14] Covey, *The Speed of Trust*, 2006, Page 199

Part Five: Networking & Profiling the Customer

Chapter 15
The Power of Smart Networking

Once you've created an opportunity to meet new people, establish yourself as an 'information hub' – a key role of any good networker.[1]

Networking. In today's world it's an inescapable necessity that businesses have an IT expert available. We all know that every computer needs to be connected and that the entire network needs to function properly. When the network goes down, the workflow ceases.

People who are serious about customer relationships bring the same dedication as an IT expert. They are dedicated to three things. First, staying connected with their current customers. Second, using their network of current customers to meet new customers. And third, strategically networking with the Govies.

Guy Kawasaki suggests you need to be like Jerry McGuire, a connected agent with a massive list of contacts. For various reasons, it's easy to resist the idea of growing a large network. Not everyone is naturally wired to want to grow an ever-increasing network of connections or friendships. Others feel like they are too busy to grow their network. And many feel that trying to grow their network is self-serving and somehow sleazy.

If you feel that way, it's useful to note Adam Grant's perspective on networking.

"On the one hand, the very notion of networking often has negative connotations. When we meet a new person who expresses enthusiasm about connecting, we frequently wonder whether he's acting friendly because he's genuinely interested in a relationship that will benefit both of us, or because he wants something from us. At some point in your life, you've probably experienced the frustration of dealing with slick schmoozer's who are nice to your face when they want a favor, but end up stabbing you in the back – or simply ignoring you – after they got what they want. This faker style of networking casts the entire enterprise as Machiavellian, a self-serving activity in which people make connections for the sole purpose of advancing their own interests. On the other hand, givers and matchers often see networking as an appealing way to connect with new people and ideas. We meet many people throughout our professional and personal lives, and since we all have different knowledge and resources, it makes sense to turn to these people to exchange help, advice, and introductions.

"By developing a strong network, people can gain invaluable access to knowledge, expertise, and influence. Extensive research demonstrates that people with rich networks achieve higher performance ratings, get promoted faster, and earn more money."[2]

It's easy to overlook the mathematical power of smart networking, even with one individual at a time.

"Networks facilitate exponential growth – in other words, if five of your customers each tell three people about you, and if each of them just tells one other – you've suddenly reached 30 potential new customers. This is why I believe you should make it a habit of giving away good ideas to customers instead of hoarding them."[3]

Metcalfe's law is also worth noting. Robert C. Metcalfe was the co-inventor of the Ethernet. The law states that the value of a network is proportional to the square of the number of users. Similarly, your network goes up exponentially as it expands.

The Law of 250 brings home the power of a network to exponentially build relationships.

"The great automobile salesperson, Joe Girard, coined the Law of 250, which says that on average, every person has about 250 people in his life who would show up at his wedding or funeral. Joe concluded that if he treated one customer poorly, he had lost not one sale but a potential of 250 sales. On the other hand, he reasoned, if he treated that same person well, he had just had a positive influence on 250 people, and not just on one.

"Which means that every single time you meet one new person and cultivate a relationship with that person to the point where they know, like, and trust you, you have just increased your own personal sphere of influence not by one but by a potential 250 at least, and likely a great many more."[4]

Even the inimitable Yogi Berra demonstrated the importance of networking when he said, "Always go to other people's funerals, otherwise, they won't come to yours."

Okay, back to more serious content.

"The Dunbar number is another series of metrics about networking. The best known, a hundred and fifty (150), is the number of people we call casual friends – the people, say, you'd invite to a large party. (In reality, it's a range of a hundred at the low end and up to two hundred for the more social of us.)

"From there, through qualitative interviews coupled with analysis of experimental and survey data, Dunbar discovered that the number grows and decreases according to a precise formula, roughly a "rule of three." The next step down, fifty (50), is the number of people we call close friends – perhaps the people you'd invite to a group dinner. You see them often, but not so much that you consider them to be true intimates. Then there's the circle of fifteen: the friends that you can turn to for sympathy when you need it, the ones you can confide in about most things. The most intimate Dunbar number, five, is your close support group. These are your best friends (and often family members.)

"On the flipside, groups can extend to five hundred, the acquaintance level, and to fifteen hundred, the absolute limit – the people for whom you can put a name to a face. While the group sizes are relatively stable, their composition can be fluid. Your five today may not be your five next week; people drift among layers and sometimes fall out of them altogether."[5]

In government customer relationships, I suspect the numbers would be smaller, making each relationship even more valuable. Here are the postulated Barrett numbers:

- Casual Customers = 45
- Close Customers = 15
- Close Support Group = 3

Tips for Smart Networking

"Everyone goes to a networking event to better themselves in some way or another. Make sure you're prepared to help someone else get better."[6]

"It seems counterintuitive, but the more altruistic your attitude, the more benefits you gain from the relationship," writes LinkedIn founder Reid Hoffman. "If you set out to help others," he explains, "you rapidly reinforce your own reputation and expand your universe of possibilities."[7]

Here is some additional high-level guidance:

"Don't keep score: It's never simply about getting what you want. It's about getting what you want and making sure that the people who are important to you get what they want, too."[8]

"Ping constantly: The ins and outs of reaching out to those in your circle of contacts all the time – not just when you need something."[9]

"That's what I mean by connecting. It's a constant process of giving and receiving – of asking for and offering help. By putting people in contact with one another, by giving your time and expertise and sharing them freely, the pie gets bigger for everyone."[10]

It has been said that the best time to borrow money from a bank is when you don't need it. Likewise, connect with people when you don't need anything. Set up what Adam Grant, in his book, *Give and Take,* calls "Reciprocity Rings." Stay in touch with people. Connect with them. Look for ways to help them without expecting anything in return. And keep in mind:

"To be successful at networking, refrain from becoming a walking, talking, marketing brochure and get it through your thick skull that nobody cares about you or what you have to say. They want to talk about themselves. You don't go to networking events to sell. You're not there to set appointments, get leads or close business. You are there to create connections with other people. You get those other things after the connections are established. There should be no quid pro quo attached to your conversations."[11]

Stay Connected

"If 80% of success is, as Woody Allen once said, just showing up, then 80% of building and maintaining relationships is just staying in touch. It's called 'pinging.' It's a quick, casual greeting, and it can be done in any number of creative ways. Once you develop your own style, you'll find it easier to stay in touch with more people than you ever dreamed of in less time than you ever imagined."[12]

You must be present to win: this popular expression to win raffles is also useful to win business. In the rapid rhythm of daily life, it's easy to forget to be present and connect with others. If that has happened to you, follow Gitomer's advice: "Take a moment and list your top ten most powerful connections (the people who can make things happen, and make things happen for you.) Then ask yourself, 'What have I done for these people lately?'"[13]

To stay connected, set up a tickler system to reconnect every 30 or 60 days.

Finally, here are four requests of your customers:

1. *Ask customers to share your work. Ask if they would forward your briefing or white paper to their team and others who could be interested.*

2. *Who else should I talk to? Would you mind sending them an email to make the contact?*

3. *Is there someone else that could benefit from this briefing? Would you sponsor me to see General X (or Admiral Y)?*

4. *Can I come back in 30 days to share an update on XYZ?*

In closing, remember what Calvin Coolidge said, *"No person was ever honored for what he received. Honor has been the reward for what he gave."* Network to serve more, help more, and give more.

[1] Ferrazzi, *Never Eat Alone*, 2005, Page 120
[2] Grant, *Give and Take*, 2013, Page 30
[3] Sobel, *Making Rain*, 2003, Page 149
[4] Burg and Mann, *Go-Givers Sell More*, 2010, Page 84
[5] http://www.newyorker.com/science/maria-konnikova/social-media-affect-math-dunbar-number-friendships
[6] Jeffrey Gitomer, *Little Black Book of Connections* (Austin: Bard Press, 2006.)
[7] Grant, *Give and Take*, 2013, Page 31
[8] Ferrazzi and Raz, *Never Eat Alone*, 2005, Inside Jacket Cover
[9] Ibid
[10] Ferrazzi and Raz, *Never Eat Alone*, 2005, Page 15
[11] Blount, Fanatical Prospecting, 2015, Page 101
[12] Ferrazzi, *Never Eat Alone*, 2005, Page 181
[13] Jeffrey Gitomer, *Little Black Book of Connections*, 2006, Page 6

Chapter 16
The Art of Playing Chess

There is no elevator to success. You have to take the stairs.[1]

When developing customer relationships, you have to *take the stairs*. This takes grit, patience and persistence. It also requires you to understand two things: *who* in your organization should be running up the stairs and which customer counterpart should they be running to meet. It is like the game of chess.

 David Pugh, in *Powerful Proposals*, leverages a chess analogy for the capture process. He says to start by matching pieces: use kings on kings, knights on knights, and pawns on pawns. Work on relationships at all levels. Connect with key high-level decision-makers and influencers so that unfiltered messages can be transmitted between kings or queens talking to other kings or queens.

At the same time, make sure you're meeting with adjacent *Knights, Bishops and Rooks.* "Good players are always looking for ways to make their pieces as active as possible. Knights need to find advanced support points, Bishops need open diagonals, and open lanes must be created for your Rooks."[2] The government likes having clear lines of communications and it's smart to have counterparts that form bonds.

Identify a one-for-one assignment of your people to government personnel without dismissing anyone. For example, the cost analysts or

RMS (Reliability, Maintainability, and Supportability) folks are often discounted as not worthy of a SME-to-SME meeting. Wrong! During the evaluation, these folks get a vote. And you can be sure they will be pre-biased toward you if you took the time to meet with them and start a relationship early.

The same is true for your program manager (PM) and chief engineer. These are the two key people that the Source Selection team wants to become familiar with. If the first time the customer meets the PM and chief engineer is at the orals, you're on a path to lose. Winning companies assign these roles early and then build a relationship with the customer. (Ironically, the PM is often the *last* person the customer meets and the person in that role often changes several times.)

Continuing with David Pugh's insights, you must meet with the customers/evaluators/influencers at different organizational levels and different functions. You must foster and nurture relationships horizontally across multiple functions and vertically up and down the chains of command.

This fostering needs to be an ongoing process because of the relentless churn of government customers. The government frequently exercises one of the 3Rs with their personnel: Rotated, Re-assigned, or Retired (either voluntary or encouraged.) As such, there is always a risk of your key allies leaving.

To mitigate this risk, consider a 3x3 approach: Network at three levels vertically up and down the chain of command while networking horizontally across three functional disciplines such as program management, engineering, cost analyst, contracts, etc. Make it your aim to have layered relationships resulting in tight relationships at multiple levels.

Another strong analogy to reinforce this 3x3 approach is to develop a "zipper up" plan. "You need to 'zipper up' the relationship with your clients. What you want is to have many ties to the client, many people at your company who have connections with people who work at the client. It creates a 'zippering' effect. It's very hard to tear a zipper apart. The more connections you have with the client—the tighter the relationship—the more likely it is that you're going to keep the client."[3]

This Chess Game is a Contact Sport

Relationship building is a contact sport. Without customer contact, no preference is created and no relationship moves to the right on the Relationship Continuum. To win in this contact sport, you need a specific and workable plan.

There are many names for plans – contact plan, call plan, customer engagement plan, customer influence plan, customer map, and customer community contact plan.

In my view a CRP (Customer Relationship Plan) is a superset of these that serves three functions:

1. It categorizes people involved in the acquisition.

2. It is action-oriented.

3. It maps personality profiles and messaging.

A simple template is shown below. It should be aggressively managed and be a *living* document.

Customer Relationship Plan Example

Customer Name/Org	Decision Role	DISC®/ MBTI® Profile	Hot Buttons	Relationship Status	Who & When?	Message
LTC Jones/SPO	SSEB	D/ ENTP	Data	Coach	VP Eng. 2/29	Low risk
	SSA			Lean Away		
	SSAC			Coach		
	Influencer			Anti-Sponsor		
	User			Neutral		
	PCO			Lean to you		

Often even engineering contractors don't take a disciplined approach to designing a Customer Relationship Plan. Common missed opportunities include:

- Over-meeting with the people that like you and are already *in your corner*. It feels good, but you must meet with distractors too.

- Ignoring the power dimension and not getting to the people who have decision influence over *this* source selection decision. For example, you could meet with a 4-star general, but if he's out of the loop and not connected, nothing will happen except you will have an overinflated opinion of your RTW (Relationships That Win) status.

- Meeting with followers rather than the opinion leaders.

To avoid these common pitfalls, utilize the sample 2x2 RTW (Relationships That Win) Matrix below. It provides two steps to increase your Pwin (Probability of Win):

Step 1. Objectively plot the real voters (SSA, SSAC, SSEB) by names on this matrix.

Step 2. Work an action plan to move your focus UP and to the RIGHT.

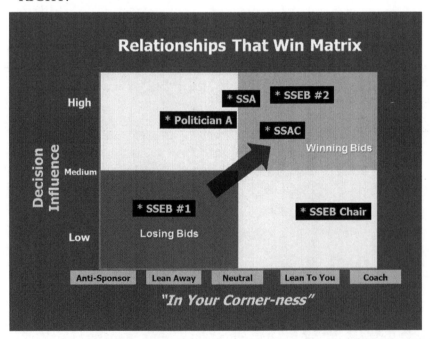

The Y-axis or *Decision Influence* factor plots how much clout each voter has. The author Rick Page has an insightful term for the evaluation committee process; he calls it *algebraic democracy*. While some votes count x, others count 5x since they have disproportionately more decision influence.

The X-axis is the degree of *In Your Corner-ness* that spans from an anti-sponsor that can submarine your efforts to a strategic coach that helps you into the winner's circle.

For technical folks seeking an equation, we can further quantify:

$$D(R) \times F(R) \times DI = \textbf{Probability of Win}$$

Where:

- D(R) = Depth of Relationship
- F(R) = Frequency of Relationship
- DI = Decision Influence

Jeb Blount correctly states, "Sales is a blend of art and science. The art is influencing people to make commitments. The science is influencing the right people."[4] Your job is to find the right people, the opinion leaders who bias the rest. (Be aware that Source Selection evaluators are often different from the day-to-day program implementers.)

To build customer advocacy, develop a customer contact strategy. In the process, be cognizant of these realities:

1. Customer is plural and not monolithic. There is no one *voice of the customer*. In selling to the government, it's a choir of voices, not a soloist. For example, each DoD service has multiple user commands, requirements generators, acquisition buyers, and the budget folks in the Pentagon.

2. People often have FRS (False Relationship Syndrome) where they overestimate their relationship and perceived knowledge. Having a meal or a drink with a customer is not a relationship. Don't overestimate your relationship like the capture manager who told me, "We have tremendous customer insight – look at all these industry day charts!"

   a. Know the difference between real and faked behavior.

   b. Know the difference between politeness and interest.

   c. Know the difference between access and influence.

    d. Know the difference between humoring you and leaning into the conversation.

3. Mitigate an all too common dreaded scenario. You've built a strong relationship with the SSEB chair, then boom! Right before the proposal evaluation starts, she gets transferred. There is no time to build a new relationship and the door is slammed closed. Insure against this disaster by paying a small insurance premium to foster a breadth of relationships. It will pay dividends.

4. Assign relationship owners. In basketball there are two kinds of defense: zone and man-to-man. Zone defense doesn't work for relationships. You must play person-to-person and have assigned (and written down) relationship owners.

5. Use referrals, don't cold call. Cold calling is dead (not sure it was ever really alive). Here is a notable factoid regarding C-level executives: "Important statistics to remember: 92% of C-level executives never respond to e-mail blasts or cold calls, but 84% of prospects do respond when referred by coworkers or customers."[5] I would argue that the never respond option is even more true for general officers and federal customers.

Executive Relationships = Kings and Queens

Executive relationships are incredibly critical but easily overlooked because of schedule constraints and other priorities. The reality is that if you are an executive, you cannot be a desk jockey. Follow the advice of Stanford entrepreneurship professor Steve Brandt, *Get out of the building.* Your counterparts need to get to know you.

"From a customer's viewpoint, if you consider yourself customer-focused but you are a senior executive who doesn't like spending time with key customers, then your lack of commitment will be evident on your calendar – and by your absence in my office. Conversely, if you are excited about and engaged by serving customers, your enthusiasm will show in how you behave toward me. It will be evident not only in your words but in the fact that you do more probing to understand my needs, bring me more ideas, take more time to help me, and go out of your way to take the extra steps that someone less committed to serving customers won't take."[6]

When it comes to forging smart customer relationships, I encourage senior executives to recognize the difference between being an empty suit versus a suitor.

A suitor is a person who pursues a relationship with another person with the goal of marriage. Let's tweak that definition to a contractor who pursues a customer relationship with a goal of doing quality business. To acronym-ize (a popular thing to do in DoD) aim to be a SUIT-R (pronounced suitor) meaning you See, Understand, and Improve The Relationships.

Your executives should be SUIT-Rs and pair up by "Customer Mapping" so they have responsibility of *owning* the relationship. The CEO/president and the VP of BD should make the assignments, and the progress should be tracked at staff meetings and Customer Relationship Plan reviews. The goal is to see the same face as much as possible. You have to have meaningful meetings at least twice per year – with the goal of quarterly.

The ideal customer visit is one when you have an open-ended return flight; you leave when you have advanced your relationship. Make it your priority to increase your business rhythm and frequency of leadership meetings. One VP at a top defense contractor books airline tickets to D.C. and goes to the Pentagon one day *every* month. His BD team is responsible to arrange the meetings, but he shows up like clockwork.

I suggest you buy airline shuttle tickets so you aren't hurried and have more flexibility to catch the next flight. Customers can tell when your main focus is on getting home.

Keeping Executive Focus

It's amazing how data-centric companies are. With big data analytic approaches such as Six Sigma and SAP or Oracle, companies collect and analyze reams of data. But when it comes to data on senior customer relationships, the dashboard indicators are seriously lacking.

Even if your BD team uses a CRM (Customer Relationship Management) tool like Salesforce, executives typically don't use these. So here are five simple metrics to assess executive focus:

1. Check the executive team's monthly calendar and calculate the ratio of internal vs. external meetings. If the ratio is too internally focused, set aside time for more customer meetings.

2. Check the number of internal briefing reviews that are for internal senior executives vs. the number of dry runs for external customer briefings.

3. Check the lobby sign-in sheet to see how many customers have come to your place.

4. At staff meetings, estimate what percentage of the activities respond to customer actions.

5. Fence off a day for no internal meetings. For example, No Meeting Wednesday (NMW) is an integral part of Asana's culture and something everyone looks forward to. Call it Customer Relationships Day and time-block it on the calendar.

Status your progress frequently to make sure these customer meetings are happening *and* producing two-way communications. As George Bernard Shaw said, "The greatest problem in communication is the illusion that it has been accomplished."

At senior staff meetings ask, "Who did you see last week and who are you seeing this week? Can we review the 30-day Customer Relationship Plan?" At staff meetings, put up photos of senior customers and see who knows their names and the most interesting details about them. Evaluate how many frequent flyer and hotel points your executive team accrues from customer visits. (Don't count internal meetings at other facilities, off-sites or supplier/partner visits.)

Know Your Vital Few

"During the World War II era, a quality guru, Joseph Juran, observed that most product quality problems came from just a few products. He referred to this as "the phenomenon of the *vital few and the trivial many*." This was a rediscovery of what the Italian economist Vilfredo Pareto observed in the 80/20% rule – namely there appeared to be a fundamental imbalance in life tending to cause a lot to come from a little."[7]

The principle of the vital few also pertains to customer relationships.

There are a few individuals that are key counterparts to those in your organization. As in chess, match your team up and get serious about your customer contact plan. Make a concerted effort to identify and move key players on the Relationships That Win Matrix.

In the world of government contracts, it is a common default mode for organizations to be laser-focused on products. Make it your priority to be equally focused on the art of playing chess: *get your people in front of their customer counterpart.* And begin this process well before the RFP hits the street.

"Having the right relationships also depends on pre-selling your team. You build credibility, in part, by having the right team to serve the customer's needs. It's imperative to introduce that team not only before you submit your proposal but also before the customer releases a bid request. When they read about your proposed team in your proposal, customers should think of them as old friends."[8]

Don't forget:

1. Relationship building is a contact sport.

2. You can fake caring, but you can't fake showing up.

3. Relationships started early and done well build trust and create preference.

4. Learn to play chess.

Mindset Tips:

✓ Aggressively play chess by executing a Customer Relationship Plan.

✓ Track my five metrics to improve your executive to senior customer relationships.

✓ Calculate the degree of influence and decision-making authority using the 2x2 Relationships That Win Matrix and move relationships up and to the right.

[1] Wolfgang Riebe
[2] Bacon & Pugh, *Winning Behavior*, 2003, Page 337
[3] http://www.jdsupra.com/legalnews/zipper-up-your-clients-relationships-t-66638/
[4] Blount, *Fanatical Prospecting*, 2015, Page 105
[5] Walker, *The Customer Centric Selling Field Guide to Prospecting and Business Development*, 2013, Page 23
[6] Bacon & Pugh, *Winning Behavior*, 2003, Page 34
[7] Reilly, *Value Added Selling*, 2010, Page 63
[8] Bacon, 2002

Chapter 17 Profiles of Evaluators

Does the customer know us, our management team, our past performance, our reputation for doing outstanding work, etc., and is there a sense that the customer is favorable to our performing the work.[1]

By now, you know that customers buy you and your team. You have to pass the personal chemistry test, not just the technology exam.

This test extends to the evaluators, no matter how large or small the contract. It matters if you're working on a huge job worth hundreds of billions like the Joint Strike Fighter or KC-46 military airlift contract. And it matters if you're working a small $50K SBIR (Small Business Innovation Research) award or a DARPA contract where they rely on the PI (Principle Investigator) for evaluation insights. Across the board, we need to understand the evaluators and what customers buy.

What Customers Buy

As you play chess at all levels and all functions, there is a fundamental question that you must answer before you spend too much on airfare: *What do customers buy?*

Jay Conrad Levinson developed a list of "Golden Rules to Guide Your Thinking" that helps answer this question. Included below is the applicable subset that maps to government contracting.

- They buy *benefits* and not features.

- They buy *promises* you make.

- They buy the promises they want *personally* fulfilled.

- They buy your *credibility* – or don't buy if you lack it.

- They buy *solutions* to their problems.

- They buy *you,* your *employees,* and your *service.*

- They buy your *guarantee, reputation,* and *good name.*

- They buy *other people's opinions* of your business.

- They buy *expectations* based upon your marketing.

- They buy *believable* claims, not simply honest claims.

- They buy the *consistency* they have seen you exhibit.

- They buy *value* – which is not the same as price.

- They buy *freedom from risk.*

- They buy *acceptance by others* of your goods and services.

- They buy *certainty.*

- They buy *convenience* in buying, paying and lots more.

- They buy *respect* for their own ideas and personality.

- They buy your *identity* as conveyed by your marketing.

- They buy *clarity* – if they don't understand they don't buy.

- They buy *honesty* – one dishonest word means no sale.

- They buy *comfort,* offerings that fit their comfort zone.

- They buy *success* – your success, which can lead to theirs.[2]

Take a moment to review the list and note how many of the guidelines are relationship based rather than product based. It's valuable to keep them in mind when dealing with evaluators in the selection process.

"The government sets up an evaluation team for each bid, usually different persons from the battery of specialists and negotiators that confronted a company in initial bid discussion. They bring their own prejudices, points of view, and foibles – which may or may not be the same as those of the negotiators who wrangled over proposal minutiae. All the problems of the commercial buying committee are encountered. All the same preselling strategies apply. The difference is that in government marketing the contractor usually has no idea just who is on the evaluation team, hence the importance of selling the entire agency on the value of the project – those above and those below the project office."[3]

The key members of Source Selection* are the SSA (Source Selection Authority), SSAC (Source Selection Advisory Council), and the SSEB (Source Selection Evaluation Board) see footnote if you want definitions. Of the 20 to 30 people on a large SSEB, there are typically three to five real players and opinion leaders. Find them early (you will have to make an educated guess) and build a relationship to earn their trust and vet your solution.

---

* Here are the roles of each member:
SSA
- The SSA is the individual designated to make the best-value decision.
- Select the source whose proposal offers the best value to the Government in accordance with evaluation-established criteria in Section M evaluation criteria.

SSAC
- The SSA establishes an SSAC to gain access to functional area expertise to provide the support the SSA requires throughout the source selection process.
- Review the evaluation results of the SSEB to ensure the evaluation process follows the evaluation criteria and the ratings are appropriately and consistently applied.
- Consolidate the advice and recommendations from the SSAC into a written comparative analysis and recommendation for use by the SSA.
- In making the best-value decision. Ensure that minority opinions within the SSAC are documented and included within the comparative analysis.

SSEB
The SSEB is comprised of a Chairperson and Evaluators (also known as SSEB Members.) Frequently, the SSEB Members will be organized into functional teams corresponding to the specific evaluation criteria (e.g., Technical Team, Past Performance Team, Cost Team, etc.) In those instances, a Functional Team Lead may be utilized to consolidate the evaluation findings of the team and serve as the primary team representative to the SSEB Chair. Use of non-Government personnel as voting members of the SSEB is prohibited. The SSEB is chartered to conduct a comprehensive review and evaluation of proposals against the solicitation requirements and the approved evaluation criteria.
Source: Source Selection Procedures, Department of Defense, Defense Federal Acquisition Regulation Supplement Procedures, Guidance and Information Subpart 215.3 – Source Selection March 31, 2016.

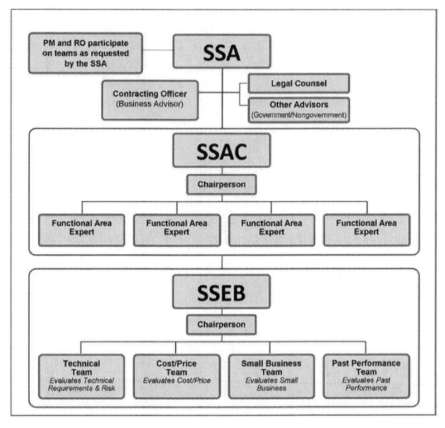

Reference: DoD Source Selection Procedure, March 31, 2016.

The military uses an IFF system to Identify Friend or Foe. You will need your own IFF when determining an advocate or a bad-vocate. Within the evaluators, there are three primary types of relationships in the hierarchy of *Coach, Neutral* and *Anti-Sponsor*. Neutral is obvious, but let's delve into the others.

Coach

"A coach describes someone inside the customer organization who wants your solution, likes you, and coaches you on how to navigate through the sticky wickets. The coach has to respect you, and be respected by the other buying influences in the organization as it relates to the specific pursuit that you are chasing. You have to actively work on developing at least one coach in the customer organization."[4]

Within the appropriate limits, your strong Govie coaches and advocates act as BD (Business Development) for your company. When relationships become strong, the Govies become an extension of your BD team. This has a two-fold force multiplier effect. First, they are added resources and lobby for you when you're not there. Second, they have infinitely more credibility when they vouch for you to other Govies.

The power of a coach was recently made clear to a colleague of mine. He had an intense discussion with a sales veteran who confided that he could predict a win or a loss with high confidence. How? His predictive abilities had nothing to do with product, technology or even past performance; it was whether or not he had a coach.

When the doors are closed and the evaluation team is sequestered, you need someone on the inside. The insider helps explain your position and provides an EN (Evaluation Notice) to help guide you to provide the right data. The support cannot be overtly blatant or it can often be discounted.

Coaches need credibility and must be willing to support you and provide insight.

"Credibility. Coaches must have major influence, and often actual decision-making authority, in the Large Account sometimes even beyond your chosen Field of Play. Good Coaches must have high credibility with senior leaders and be respected at all levels of the hierarchy. Without that credibility they could never get the coaching data that you need.

"Support. Coaches are ready, willing, and able to actively support your efforts. Why isn't important. Whether the reasons are rational or emotional, political or professional, the Coach sees a personal win in promoting your tenancy. Coaches must be behind not just the individual transactions or initiatives; they must give advice and guidance on the relationship as a whole and must want you in the account for the long term.

"Insight. Third, Coaches are able to support your long-term tenancy because they can provide you the kind of insight that only insiders have."[5]

Coaches need to have some gravitas and not be what I refer to as a *"BBQ Bud."*

What is a Barbeque Bud? It's a relationship that is primarily social and lacks a serious professional component. The symptoms are that you attend BBQs or parties together, dine together, and maybe even have a tight bond of formerly being in the service together. These experiences create the false impression that this "bud" is in your corner.

Being buds with a customer doesn't mean that he or she likes your program manager or that their management believes in your company or solution. Also, others may be aware of this social bud bias and discount the opinions or advocacy of the bud. While close relationships are good and having a "Bud" in your hand can help while networking, make sure you also have candid professional dialogues.

Anti-Sponsor

Anti-Sponsors are the people that can obstruct or submarine your company or system. If they are blatantly biased or negative, your coach inside may be able to neutralize them. Or they may be deemed prejudiced against you, which can result in others discounting their opinions. Like a biased juror, they may not be selected to be part of the decision team.

"Like a Coach, an Anti-Sponsor is credible to the buying organization. He or she has authority that may exert influence on how its key players are thinking. And that's the danger, because the Anti-Sponsor, by definition, wants you *out* or someone or something else in. Whatever else he or she may do, as far as you're concerned the Anti-Sponsor's role is to *negate your efforts* to improve your position."[6]

"Assessment of individual personalities is very important to winning. Although no single person in the customer organization can assure that you win, there is usually one person who can have a sufficiently negative influence to assure you lose. That is the 'weak link' in your bid chain."[7]

In the critical moments of award decisions, a Coach and an Anti-Sponsor can make a pivotal difference. Remember, to maximize the one and minimize the other. Pay attention to the source selection organization.

> *Mindset Tips:*
>
> ✓ Understand the government's buying process. Synthesize the names of the SSA, SSAC, and SSEB.
>
> ✓ Of the 20 to 30 people on the Source Selection Evaluation Board, there are typically three to five real players and opinion leaders. Find them early and build a relationship to earn their trust and vet your solution.
>
> ✓ Create Coaches and be aware and beware of Anti-Sponsors.

---

[1] Bob Lohfeld

[2] Jay Conrad Levinson, *Guerrilla Marketing Excellence: The 50 Golden Rules for Small-Business Success*

[3] Robertson, *Selling to the Federal Government*, 1979, Pages 124-125

[4] Smotrova-Taylor, *How to Get Government Contracts*, 2012, Page 97

[5] Miller, Heiman and Tuleja, *The New Successful Large Account Management*, 2005, Page 80-81

[6] Miller, Heiman and Tuleja, *The New Successful Large Account Management*, 2005, Page 82

[7] Kaplan, *Acquiring Major Systems Contracts*, 1988, Page 26

Part Six: Ready, Set, Meet with Govies

Chapter 18 Relationships are for Engineers Too

Get more face time. Be eyeball-to-eyeball. Connect your engineers to the customer's engineers.

Winning a complex procurement is not a solo mission for the business development function. It also entails more than having relationships with flag officers. Winning is a team sport that requires a smart relationship between your engineers and the customer's SMEs (Subject Matter Experts.)

In this chapter, we will zoom in on why engineers are a critical part of the team. We will also examine why we are reluctant to bring some engineers to customer meetings. Finally, we will look at how to enhance the engineer's relationship with customers.

Bottom line up front: With respect to your lead engineers, bring them, prep them, and connect them with the customer's engineers. The relationship between your engineers and the customers' SMEs is vital.

As Bob Lohfeld, head of Lohfeld Consulting, says:

"We hear all the time that it's difficult to get access to customers, yet companies are still doing it successfully, and we know that access is a strong predictor of future bid success. Double down on your efforts to establish relationships with customers on both the mission and acquisition sides of the government organization. As you map out your call campaign, if you have influential senior staff in your organization who know the customer (maybe former government senior staff), make sure they have a chance to visit, and be sure to include your solution lead/architect and your program manager in your call plan. It shouldn't just be BD making customer calls. Engage your teammates too."[1]

Should I Bring My Engineer?

The Myth-Busters memo states the answer clearly: "In meetings with government technical personnel, it's far more valuable for you to bring subject matter experts to the meeting rather than focusing on the sales pitch."[2]

Most technical civilians and SETA[3] contracts want to talk to a real engineer (not a BD/sales person that plays one and may bluff a bit.) They value being on a first name basis with your top two or three engineers. Their big questions are:

- Who are your engineers?

- Can they do the job?

- Are they arrogant? (Your engineers may think they have a patent on arrogance! Some do.)

- Will they belittle me and make me feel like a technical lightweight or help me and make me look smart?

- What would it be like to tackle our biggest challenges with them?

Select a chief engineer who understands mission and operational analysis so his first challenge will be finding the customer's MIRs (Most Important Requirements.) Select one who listens exceptionally well and can discuss trade-offs and multiple solutions rather than a single product. Select one that the technical customers highly respect and want to work with.

The chief engineer should:

- Love to explain and teach without being arrogant or lecturing. (The secret is to educate with modesty rather than arrogance.)

- Work trade study choices to draw out customer preferences.

- Focus on the customer's problem rather than selling your products.

It's essential to know the customer's engineers and grasp their priorities and pain. In a final competition, one contractor received a "Good" (Purple) proposal score; they had lots of strengths, only minor weaknesses and the lowest price. Yet they lost. Why? They answered the RFP perfectly but missed the Real Felt Pain completely. The winner won with a huge premium of over 20% higher price for additional operational capability. They listened hard. That is the key to Billion Dollar Mindsets. It pays to know the customer's chief engineers intimately so you can maximize their often unwritten value proposition. Your reward will be a profitable win.

So Why the Fear of Bringing the Engineer?

When it comes to having brilliant engineers meet with the customer, it's comical to see the concern some contractors have about the meeting. Here are some common concerns, real and imagined:

1. **The "Data Dump"** – Also known as the *curse of knowledge*, where engineers think they have to provide reams of technical information to persuade the customer. There is an engineering tendency to provide excessive amounts of background and extraneous details.

"Avoid the *Curse of Knowledge* (a common disease for many engineers)

Drowning people in detail.

Almost everywhere I go I come across people who think the best way to convince and persuade people over a particular argument is to tell them everything they know on the subject. They mistakenly believe, 'If I bombard you with enough facts you're bound to submit to my way of thinking.'

Wrong.

People who are drowning in detail are usually gasping for insight."[4]

2. **Technical Arrogance** – Many engineers have competed their entire careers to be the best; they like to show their technical know-how. When with the customer, they pride themselves on winning the argument but forget the importance of a dialogue.

Be aware that your technical team can be viewed as coveted heroes with one customer and zeros by another. Company X had a team of highly talented senior engineers. When working with prime customers, they were revered. They were smart, highly confident and carried the technical load. These customers deferred all technical decisions to this team and it was a win-win relationship.

Unfortunately, when trying to win a contract with a new technical customer, these exact same engineers were viewed as arrogant and difficult to work with. And, since the customer SMEs were on the SSEB, they were among the scorers. The engineer-to-engineer relationships can be paramount to winning or losing. It pays to know how you are being perceived by your customer.

3. **Problem Focus** – Engineers love problems. If a system works brilliantly 99.9% of the time, they will make a deep-dive esoteric diagnosis of the 0.1%!

4. **Risk Aversion** – They are risk averse and can be pessimistic. Consequently, they under promise on performance. They forget that if you want to earn business you must promise big and deliver even bigger.

5. **Introversion** – As the old joke goes: "What is the difference between an introverted and extroverted engineer?" The answer, "When talking, the introvert looks at *his* own shoes. The extrovert looks at *your* shoes." Clever, but Adam Grant, the brilliant researcher from the University of Pennsylvania, reminds introverts of the value of learning to become slightly more outgoing and engaging. (He also suggests the value of extroverts learning to throttle back their extroversion when speaking with others.)

6. **Logos Driven** – Engineers are generally logos (fact-based logic) driven. As a result, they often prefer to present details of *how* the watch works, not *what it does*. In the process, using communication techniques such as analogies, metaphors, stories, and sound bites that invoke emotion are not part of their engineering mindset.

There's one last concern that some people have when deciding whether or not to bring their engineer to meet with the customer. They fear the engineer will say too much or tell the truth.

You might recall the riveting scene from *A Few Good Men* when the colonel, played by Jack Nicholson, declares, "You can't handle the truth." The *Billion Dollar Mindsets* phrase is slightly different in that *you must handle the truth.* You must get to the truth early.

A truth-telling engineer is necessary and valuable. The customer will call this trusted engineer when they have a problem because they know they will be told the ground truth. It's a great tag team to have an "Honest Abe" technical truth-teller along with a BD person. You will notice the customer engineers looking to Abe to substantiate what the BD person is saying. Trust is built when Abe contradicts or reigns in the BD person.

Back to the original question: Should I bring my engineer? Again, yes. And if for some reason you have to fly solo without your chief engineer, then you may have to *phone a friend* from the meeting. If the meeting gets technical and there's a thirst for more technical discussion, don't say I'll get back to you. Respond real-time by calling back to your company and closing the loop. The customer will like your responsiveness to their interests.

Start putting your engineers in front of the customer as early as possible. You *must* pre-sell key engineers. The technical relationship between your chief engineer and the SSEB (Source Selection Evaluation Board) technical chairperson is perhaps the strongest correlation to a win. The investment in this relationship has a high return and is often overlooked. Make it your goal to convert customer skeptics to champions that speak for your solution.

Engineers are trained to be analytical, almost robotic. They are rewarded for solving challenging problems and scoring high on Math SATs. If you're an engineer, you understand calculus and you know that those who grasp the fundamentals are able to excel at it.

In that vein, let's look at some fundamental concepts of smart engineering relationships. You were not taught these in your engineering classes, but if you were smart enough to learn calculus, you can learn these, too.

10 Ways to Engineer Customer Relationships

1. Listen: You might be the smartest one in the room, listen anyway.

2. Don't Debate: Resist the urge to argue. "Avoid starting with "No," "But," or "However"; the overuse of these negative qualifiers that secretly say to everyone, "I'm right. You're wrong."[5]

3. Learn: "As we grow older, our curiosity dies. The average five-year-old asks 200 questions a day. How many do you ask? Approach every situation with an intense sense of curiosity, and you will listen more."[6]

4. Don't "One-up:" "Johnny Carson is an all-time favorite entertainer. When a guest would mention a current event or piece of knowledge outside Johnny's realm, the host didn't feign understanding, try to take over the conversation, or 'one up' the guest. He simply said, 'I did not know that.' That's what you should say too."[7]

5. Keep it Simple: Avoid fancy words, jargon, and internal company lingo or techno-babble. Your customer should not need a secret decoder ring or an acronym soup to English converter.

6. Smile and Laugh: "A study at the University of Cambridge puts a value on the smile during a negotiation at a 10% increase in trust."[8] "Babies laugh, on average, four hundred times a day, and people over thirty-five laugh fewer than fifteen times a day. What happened?"[9]

7. Bring a Dental Probe: Probe for the pain. "You're digging for root-canal pain. The premise is that usually only one thing – excruciating pain – motivates someone to go through a root canal. That pain must be so intense that it hurts too much to do nothing. This is what you're probing for in the needs analysis. People change when the disadvantages of doing nothing exceed the advantages they would realize from doing something – in short, the pain is greater than the gain. When their current situation hurts more than it helps, buyers open up to change. Probe deep. Find the root canal pain."[10]

8. Remember that: ½ S = 2E: (One half the number of slides equals twice the effectiveness.) Cut the number of charts for a customer meeting to allow more discussion time. (Either delete half the slides or move them to backup.) You're trying to build trust and a technical champion not getting paid by the viewgraph!

Zero or one chart can sometimes be the right number. No one ever complained that you had too few viewgraphs, especially when you're communicating with senior customers.

9. Kickstart the Dialogue: Include your *draft requirements analysis* to engage the customer to talk and provide feedback.

10. Arrive Naked: What should you bring to a meeting? Sometimes the best thing to bring to a meeting is simply a pen and pad of paper. Bring a *single sheet of paper* as a virtual whiteboard. (For those that fear they will not have enough content, you can use both sides!) The beauty of this approach is that the customer will feel relaxed and iterate with you. The goal is to write notes or updates on your single sheet of paper. As a minimum, the paper provides guideposts to frame the discussion in the meeting.

"Learn to go in naked and to ask questions. That's the only way you're going to find the needs, problems, and opportunities of your prospects. This information will help you go back later."[11]

Bring the engineers? Absolutely. Forging a relationship between your key engineers and the SSEB engineers will pay dividends when the source selection door closes and they evaluate your technical solution. Building these relationships takes time, so start early, practice your enhanced engineering relationship skills, and remember that your customer is looking to buy capability from someone they trust. Be that person and team.

Mindset Tips:

✓ Bring your best engineer to educate, not sell.

✓ Whiteboard to listen and learn.

✓ Avoid technical arrogance and the data dump due to the curse of knowledge.

[1] Bob Lohfeld, *Here's how to tune up your business for 2016*
https://washingtontechnology.com/articles/2016/02/02/insights-lofeld-tune-up-for-2016.aspx
[2] Myth-Busting memorandum, *Addressing the Misconceptions to Improve Communication with Industry During the Acquisition Process*
[3] Systems Engineering and Technical Assistance (SETA) contractors are civilian employees or government contractors who are contracted to assist the United States Department of Defense (DoD) components, and acquisition programs.
[4] McGee, *How to Succeed With People*, 2013, Page 174
[5] Goldsmith, *What Got You Here Won't Get You There*, 2007, Page 40
[6] *Power Questions*, Page 119
[7] Rodgers, *Persuasion Equation*, 2015, Page 103
[8] Eklund, *The Sell*, 2015, Page 120
[9] Eklund, *The Sell*, 2015, Page 120
[10] Reilly, *Value Added Selling*, 2010, Page 178
[11] Wilson, *151 Quick Ideas to Get New Customers*, 2005, Page 62

Chapter 19
The Power of Smart Emotion

People buy on emotions and justify with facts.

Understanding the SSEB Scorecard for Your Proposal

To win in any sport, you need great individual or team skills. You also need to know the rules of the sport and how to keep score. The same is true of winning business with the government. You need the necessary skills to provide the products or services your customer needs. And you need to understand how the government keeps score and the rules of the game.

If you're new to the procurement world, understanding the customer's scorecard and rules for winning can be confusing. In fact, even for veterans of the industry, misunderstanding the scorecard is very common.

Many are like the capture manager who believed that winning awards was like taking a multiple-choice exam with the government. He assumed that the bidder who was rated most compliant won the contract. Upon discovering the hidden variables that impact awards, he laughed and said, "I'm a retired naval captain with a Ph.D. in physics, and frankly, understanding physics is much less complicated than the murky world of winning contracts."

In truth, understanding how to win complex contracts is not all that difficult. In the old days, U.S. Government proposals were evaluated using point scores. Each evaluator on the SSEB provided a numerical score for their section and large disparities in scores would be discussed and resolved. Then the scores were averaged, tallied by sub-factor, and weighted by importance to arrive at an overall total score. Typically, the source selection scoring was based on 1,000 points and the winning bidder won by 50 to 100 points.

Today there are no point scores. USG evaluations (per Source Selection Procedures) use color ratings and adjectival descriptions defined as:

Combined Technical/Risk Rating Method

- *Blue* = Outstanding Proposal. Indicates an exceptional approach and understanding of the requirements. Contains multiple strengths. Risk of unsuccessful performance is low.
- *Purple* = Good Proposal. Indicates a thorough approach and understanding of the requirements. Contains at least one strength. Risk of unsuccessful performance is low to moderate.
- *Green* = Acceptable Proposal. Meets requirements and indicates an adequate approach and understanding of the requirements. Risk of unsuccessful performance is no worse than moderate.
- *Yellow* = Marginal Proposal. Has not demonstrated an adequate approach and understanding of the requirements. Risk of unsuccessful performance is high.
- *Red* = Unacceptable Proposal. Does not meet requirements of the solicitation. Contains one or more deficiencies. Risk of unsuccessful performance is unacceptable. Proposal is unawardable.

The scores are a blend of technical performance (where strengths outweigh weaknesses) and a risk assessment of low, moderate, high or unacceptable.

While scoring and risk assessment sound like an impartial, quantitative process, let's revisit the government language common to many RFPs:

"While the Government will strive for maximum objectivity, the tradeoff process by its very nature is subjective; therefore, professional judgment is implicit throughout the selection process."

What influences this subjective process and these professional judgments? There are two primary influences that are imperative to understand:

- The power of human emotion in the decision-making process.

- The power of smart customer relationships to influence human emotion.

Together, human emotion and customer relationships directly impact the risk rating you receive. Evaluators can use this score to pick the people and company they want. Source selection decisions are influenced by their confidence (or lack of confidence) in you and your company. If they know you and trust you, you get the benefit of the doubt and a low risk rating. If they don't know you or trust you, the risk dial goes to moderate or high and you lose. In short, customers score you well when they feel *confident and comfortable.*

In this scoring system, emotion is a significant part of the award process and relationships are a key component of winning:

"It becomes obvious that winning business has much more to do with psychology and dealing with people than spreadsheet scores or product spec sheets. That's why, in the psychology and relationship sections, there are books about listening, caring, empathy, authenticity, vulnerability, story sharing, emotions, connecting, and relationships. *"[1]*

In some ways, SSEB members are like jurors in a high-profile court trial. We like to believe that jurors are blank slates living in a bubble to prevent them from reading, watching, or discussing any information about the trial. We want them to be unbiased and rational. Similarly, we like to believe the same things about the SSEB. Unfortunately, we need to abandon this belief. The SSEB's thinking has been influenced and shaped by their relationships... hopefully yours. This phenomenon is not unethical in any way. Rather, it's simply how humans behave. It's part of the process of decision making.

Evaluators are like everyone else: "Even when we try the rational approach – making lists of pros and cons – if it does not come out how we like, we go back and redo the list until it does."[2]

(In our daily lives, all of us know what it is to make an emotional decision that we then justify with "facts." Of course, we "notch filter" out the facts that don't support our gut emotional desire and amplify any data that supports our preconceptions and preferences. This is known as *confirmation bias*.)

Winning with Customer Relationships Pre-RFP

Relationships come before sales, before selling, and before proposing. Customer relationships are the business investments with an ROI that is reflected in your SSEB scores.

During competitions, we sometimes forget that the customer is engaged in a process called *source* selection, as opposed to system or product selection. This means that in addition to choosing a system or product, they are also selecting their preferred company and people.

Let's contrast trying to win WITHOUT smart customer relationships vs. WITH smart customer relationships. There are seven relationship difference makers:

WITHOUT Smart Customer Relationships	WITH Smart Customer Relationships
You'd better be the lowest price	Your customer will pay a premium to work with you.
You're in a sea of competitors	You're on the preferred shortlist
You may be subjectively risked up	You may be risked down
You chase false opportunities that are not qualified and never happen	You place your B&P (Bid and Proposal) funds on real opportunities
You're bidding blind, launching an unguided projectile proposal	You're providing a laser-guided precision solution that directly hits the target
Your proposal claims are suspicious and contentious	Your claims are trusted and believable
You're bidding a risky program because you don't understand the Real-Felt-Pain and the reasons behind the requirements	You're bidding smart to delight the customer and also make a profit

Positioning to Win with EMOTION

Whether meeting with your customer or submitting a proposal that resonates with the SSEB, it's important to understand, "Logic makes people think, but emotions make them **act**."[3]

Based on psychology and neuroscience, we know people buy with their heart and justify with their head.

"The people who make buying decisions in the federal government are influenced by their own biases, perceptions, and views of the world. Although the government uses an ostensibly objective scoring system to evaluate proposals, in the end it is a person who assigns the score. It's not much different from when your teachers graded you way back when. A proposal evaluator reads a submitted resume and decides the person on the resume is graded out at a score of 87 out of 100. Why not an 85 or 89? Because it's a subjective process and all procurement decisions boil down to a subjective judgment no matter how sophisticated the scoring scheme."[4]

The final award decision is made by the SSA, (The decider.) The decision announcement comes down to a sentence or two of justification from the SSA. In spite of the complex scoring and weighting of Section M (RFP evaluation criteria), the decision is nonetheless subjective. It is driven by emotion and substantiated by surgically selected data. The emotional decision is based on the strength of the relationship and the pre-RFP preference bias.

How Do You Create Preference?

To create preference, make it your goal to create an emotional connection. You can't move people to action unless you first move them with emotion. The heart comes before the head. To grasp this, allow me to go into the weeds for a few paragraphs regarding how the brain works and why emotional connections matter.

Dale Carnegie said, "When dealing with people, remember you are not dealing with creatures of logic, but with creatures of emotion, creatures bristling with prejudice and motivated by pride and vanity."[5]

Dale's insights were based on decades in a Harlem YMCA interacting with people and capturing behavior. Today's science confirms with neurological testing.

According to Hannah Devlin at the Department of Clinical Neurology, University of Oxford, functional magnetic resonance imaging (fMRI) is an approach for measuring brain activity. It works by detecting the changes in blood oxygenation and flow that occur in response to neural activity.

"Scientists using fMRI (functional magnetic resonance imaging) can scan people's brains to see exactly what areas are being activated when a subject performs a specific task, such as speaking or listening to someone else. This technology and other tools of modern science have led to an avalanche of studies in the area of communication."[6]

"Emotions create movement and action. We are persuaded by reason, but we are moved by emotion. Several studies conclude that up to 90% of the decisions we make are based on emotion. We use logic to justify our actions to ourselves and to others. Take note that emotion will always win over logic and that imagination will always win over reality. Think about talking to children about their fear of the dark, or to someone about their phobia of snakes. You know it's useless to use logic to persuade them that their thoughts and actions don't make sense. They are still convinced that there is a problem.

"Remember, logic is important, but emotion helps you catapult an otherwise dull or flat exchange to the next level."[7]

Henry M. Boettinger amplified this when he said, "Emotions and beliefs are masters, and reason their servant. Ignore emotion, and reason slumbers; trigger emotion, and reason comes rushing to help."[8]

Words can trigger an Emotional Competent Stimulus (ECS) response. For example, "Remember Martin Luther King Junior didn't inspire a generation with the phrase 'I have a strategic plan.' He had a dream. He did focus on facts, but he also stirred people's feelings."[9]

So the goal is to fire the right neurotransmitters in the minds of the evaluators.

Winning with Smart Rhetoric

It's easier to manufacture seven facts than one emotion.[10]

Persuasion theory is thousands of years old, and winning proposals includes a combination of Greek philosopher Aristotle's three main forms of rhetoric – Ethos, Pathos, and Logos. Notice that they also equate to Reputation, Emotion, and Reason.

Written proposals alone will fail to achieve these three, and they are only achievable by building relationships before the RFP. Let's delve more into Pathos.

Pathos is appeal based on emotion. This is "in the emotional state of the hearer [or evaluator]."[11] Advertisements tend to be pathos-driven.

"To handle yourself, use your head. To handle others use your heart."[12]

"Teach everyone your plan to meet the customer's emotional needs, which can be remembered with the easy formula of EN1 = Emotional Needs First."[13]

Over the years, customers selected IBM as the emotionally safe and trusted choice because of the unwritten motto: "*No one ever got fired for selecting IBM.*"

Make it your goal to create preference by connecting with your customer prior to the release of the RFP. Make them feel comfortable and confident that you are the provider they can trust with their greatest challenges.

---

[1] Bosworth and Zoldan, *What Great Salespeople Do*, 2012, Page 6

[2] Klaff, *Pitch Anything*, 2011, Page 132

[3] Scott Keyser

[4] White, *Rolling the Dice in D.C.*, 2006, Page 29

[5] Dale Carnegie, *How to Win Friends & Influence People*

[6] Gallo, *Talk Like Ted*, 2014, Page 7

[7] The Rule of Mental Balance – The Rational vs. Emotional Mind http://westsidetoastmasters.com/resources/laws_persuasion/chap14.html

[8] Duarte, *Resonate*, 2010, Page 103

[9] McGee, *How to Succeed With People*, 2013, Page 177

[10] Mark Twain, *"Life On the Mississippi"*

[11] Stanford, 2002

[12] Eleanor Roosevelt

[13] Wilson, *151 Quick Ideas to Get New Customers*, 2005, Page 55

Part Seven: Communicating with Govies

The relationship principles up to this point apply well to working with most customers. In these final chapters, I take a vertical deep-dive and zoom in with more specifics on building smart relationships with the Govies.

Chapter 20 Communications Myth-Busters

Mend government and industry relationships so that they are more collaborative and less adversarial.[1]

A pilot and co-pilot were careening down and rapidly losing altitude, destined to crash. Suddenly, the co-pilot looks over at the pilot and exclaims, "Wow, you're in a lot of trouble!"

In reality, government and industry are in the same plane, and they fly high or crash together. When viewed from a 30,000-foot perspective, something has happened to government and contractor relationships over the past dozen years. Trust has gone down, fear of protests has gone up, and stricter rules have put distance between the government and the contractors.

According to the Association of Proposal Management Professionals Survey report, communication and government to industry relationships appear at an *all-time low*. The two most critical relationship concerns they identified were:

1. "Improve government/industry communications: The OMB Myth-Busting series of memos have repeatedly emphasized the need for better communications. However, while the theory is sound, often the practice is not happening. The senior acquisition officials and 'Commander's intent' is clear about open dialogue and improving communications. Yet, in practice this remains a severe challenge. While over 90% of industry members surveyed wanted communications open to the final

RFP only 60% of Government participants saw this as a needed change. This is the largest execution gap (30%) that needs to be closed.

2. <u>Mend government and industry relationships</u> so that they are more collaborative and less adversarial: Both sides indicated they preferred more open and transparent relationships. "Sometimes we can get meetings, but they are tight-lipped, and sometimes the Government avoids industry completely."[2]

The challenge of this environment is captured by Smotrova-Taylor: "Govies try to reduce the number of opportunities for you to talk to them. They do it out of fear that something improper will happen, and they get in serious trouble."[3]

Seeing Through the Fog

Currently there is enormous confusion regarding what kind of relationship and communication between contractors and government customers is allowed by the FAR. To make sense of the rules and guidelines, Steve Charles has masterfully converted complex "FAR-isms" into straightforward English. (If you already know about the quiet period, you can skip this part.)

"There's considerable confusion about when and under what circumstance the government can talk to companies about its requirements and upcoming procurements. But the law is clear: Up until release of a request for proposals (RFPs), program managers, contracting officers and other feds are free to talk with the industry about their agencies' needs and future acquisitions.

Nothing need be off the table during such talks. By "nothing," we mean that legitimate topics of conversation include acquisition strategy, proposed contract types, terms and conditions, and acquisition planning schedules; the feasibility of a requirement, performance requirements, statements of work, and data requirements; and the suitability of the proposal instructions and evaluation criteria. The Federal Acquisition Regulations (FAR) say so.

In fact, agencies must conduct market research before releasing a solicitation for anything worth more than the simplified acquisition threshold. Legitimate market research includes one-on-one discussions with contractors. Contrary to a common myth, the government doesn't have to meet with all possible offerors to meet with just one. There is no rule requiring the government to schedule meetings with your competitors to meet with you in the time leading up to a solicitation.

Only when the solicitation is released do things change. Exchanges of information don't stop, but they become more formal and regulated. Communication must go through the contracting officer and generally must be conducted in writing. It's at this point that the law known as the Procurement Integrity Act swings into action. The Procurement Integrity Act requires contracting officers communicate identically with all potential offerors after release of a solicitation. Post-solicitation communication is in writing only. Updates, changes or instructions from the contracting officer are released publicly in the form of an amendment to the solicitation. This 'quiet period' is the likely source of the persistent myth that if the government talks to one company, it must also talk to its competitors – which is **not** the case when the government is in the pre-solicitation phase conducting market research and writing requirements. The difference between pre-solicitation and post-solicitation is as different as day from night."[4]

In light of this, it makes developing a smart relationship with your customers prior to the *quiet period* a critical imperative. From a communications perspective, imagine the difference between:

- Pre-solicitation: An informal atmosphere of collaboration, conversation, and open dialog with the PM and Engineers.

- Post-solicitation: A formal, controlled, communicate-in- writing through the PCO.

Fear of fraud is a dark cloud hanging over the head of many government customers. This legitimate concern makes them extremely careful not to violate any relationship or communication rules. But the unintended consequence of this fear is that many Govies often over-interpret the Govie-Industry communication rules.

Being aware of this, Brad Carson, DoD's former chief of personnel and readiness, astutely stated that government officials need to be better consumers of legal advice.

During a panel discussion at the Center for Strategic and International Studies, he pointed to his own experience as the Army's chief counsel:

"I remember the Secretary of the Army wanted to meet with the Boeing CEO and he asked me, 'Is this ethical to do?' I said you should meet with the CEO of Boeing, this makes complete sense," Carson recalled. "Well, there were lawyers in the Army who said, 'You can't do this, because if you meet with Boeing, you have to meet with Northrop Grumman and General Dynamics and you have to have some kind of confab.' I said, 'No, the policy needs to be you have an open door and if the CEO of General Dynamics wants to meet, you meet with them as well. But there's no requirement you have to meet with these folks in a group.' It's about overenthusiastic compliance. Too often I think senior leaders of the department feel chilled."[5]

With similar insight, Frank Kendall, Under Secretary of Defense for Acquisition, Technology and Logistics (AT&L) eloquently states, "Communicate as fully with industry as the rules allow. For some reason, we seem to have become gun shy about talking to industry. That's the wrong approach. The more we communicate our intent and priorities to industry, and the more we listen to industry concerns, the better. Up until the time a final RFP for a specific effort is released to industry, we should not overly restrict our contacts. We do have an obligation to treat all firms in the same manner – but that doesn't mean we can't have conversations with individual firms, as long as the same opportunity is available to others who want to take advantage of it."[6]

Finally, the Office of Federal Procurement Policy (OFPP) has released several Myth-Busters Memos to try to rectify these common misunderstandings of working with the federal government. They state: "Early engagement with industry has the potential to greatly improve the efficiency of the acquisition cycle." Dan Gordon, Administrator, OFPP, states, "early, frequent, and constructive engagement with industry is especially important for complex, high-risk procurements."

Look carefully at some of the Myth-Busters Memos below. Notice the government's emphasis on *the value of government-contractor communication.*

From Myth-Busters Memorandum #1

Misconception #1: "We can't meet one-on-one with a potential offeror."

Fact #1: "Government officials can meet one-on-one with potential offerors as long as no contractor receives preferential treatment. 'Prior to issuance of a solicitation, government officials – including the program manager, users or contracting officer – may meet with potential Offerors to exchange general information and conduct market research related to an acquisition. There is no requirement that meetings include all possible Offerors, nor is there a prohibition against one-on-one meetings.'"

Misconception #2: "A protest is something to be avoided at all costs – even if it means the government limits conversations with industry."

Fact #2: "Restricting communication won't prevent a protest, and limiting communication might actually increase the chance of a protest – in addition to depriving the government of potentially useful information."

(Note that some government employees who fear risk of protest feel, "there's no incentive to communicate – only risk. I don't get in trouble if I don't communicate – but I can get in trouble if I do. It's not worth the risk."[7])

Misconception #3: "The program manager already talked to industry to develop the technical requirements, so the contracting officer doesn't need to do anything else before issuing the RFP."

Fact #3: "The technical requirements are only part of the acquisition; getting feedback on terms and conditions, pricing structure, performance metrics, evaluation criteria, and contract administration matters will improve the award and implementation process."

From Myth-Busters Memorandum #2

Misconception #4: "The best way to present my company's capabilities is by marketing directly to contracting officers and/or signing them up for my mailing list."

Fact #4: "Contracting officers and program managers are often

---

inundated with general marketing material that doesn't reach the right people at the right time. As an alternative, contractors can take advantage of the various outreach sessions that agencies hold for the purpose of connecting contracting officers and program managers with companies whose skills are needed."

Misconception #5: "It's a good idea to bring only business development and marketing people to meetings with the agency's technical staff."

Fact #5: "In meetings with government technical personnel, it's far more valuable for you to bring subject matter experts to the meeting rather than focusing on the sales pitch."

Misconception #6: "Agencies generally have already determined their requirements and acquisition approach so our impact during the pre-RFP phase is limited."

Fact #6: "Early and specific industry input is valuable. Agencies generally spend a great deal of effort collecting and analyzing information about capabilities within the marketplace. The more specific you can be about what works, what doesn't, and how it can be improved, the better."

Have the Myth-Busters solved the communication problem? In a word, no. Let's finish with three additional misconceptions of my own:

Misconception #7: It's all about price and technical performance – relationships don't matter. You can't build a relationship with federal evaluators, as the FAR prohibits.

Fact #7: The FAR *encourages* dialogue with contractors.

Misconception #8: Just social relationships win.

Fact #8: Not really. There are too many people to socialize with and you don't win based on friendship.

Misconception #9: Everyone has better relationships with the customer than you and your company.

Fact #9: If you believe it, it is true.

Now that we have separated fact and myth, here are five main ethics rules that matter. They establish the boundaries and keep both sides out of trouble.

Five Ethics Rules for USG Relationships:

"Many people over-complicate the rules. The sheer magnitude and volume of the FAR pages can be daunting, so I have summarized what keeps you and your company out of trouble into five rules:

1. Don't buy gifts for U.S. Government employees [the FAR also prohibits paying for outside events (ball games, concerts...) but allows a small amount gift like a pen or coffee cup with your logo].

2. Don't buy USG meals or drinks (small dollar exception for low-cost coffee or snacks.) Place a fair market value collection box for USG folks to contribute to show your integrity.

3. Don't overtly or blatantly talk about procurement after the RFP except through the PCO. If you do, the PCO could disqualify your company for violating the FAR or OCI (Organizational Conflict of Interest.)

4. Don't ask who the Source Selection team is since the FAR prohibits it, and you don't want to compromise your relationship.

5. You can host and pay for an event at a trade show and allow USG attendees; however, it has to be open so that even your competitors could attend. Permissible conduct: Inviting a government employee having procurement responsibilities for an outing, as long as the employee pays a fair share of the costs associated with that outing."[8]

Correcting Perceptions

In the confusion of today's environment, there are negative mindsets that can cause adversarial relationships. For example, some government employees have negative views of contractors. They view them as:

- Profit mongers who care only about the money, not the mission.

- People who exaggerate just to win the work.

- People who don't care about cost overruns and schedule delays.

- People who, when their lips are moving, are lying.

Similarly, some contractors can have negative views of the government. If you're a contractor, here are some negative over-generalized government stereotypes:

- Why don't they understand profit and that defense contractors are in business with shareholders, not a charity?

- It's 4:00 PM, I'm sure the government employees are gone for the day. Why don't they work hard like us?

- They always dump the RFP on us before the holidays. Why do they seek to punish bidders?

- Why do they give us the wrong information and dates for RFP milestones?

While some of these can occasionally ring true, we need to have some empathy. Government acquisition employees have stressful and high-pressure jobs. They are often overworked and under-compensated. They are in a culture that is extremely challenging while being trained with the fear of God *not* to make a mistake in relationships with bidders. Most acquisition officials truly want to deliver equipment and services that meet the war fighters' need while maximizing value. It is precisely the same mindset of most contractors.

We need to rediscover the importance of clear communication while respecting the rules of government. We need to remember that government and industry are in the same plane: *we all fly or crash together*.

[1] APMP PIC Report, 2014

[2] APMP PIC (Procurement Improvement Committee) Report, September 2014

[3] Smotrova-Taylor, *How to Get Government Contracts*, 2012, Page 87

[4] http://www.crn.com/news/channel-programs/240164743/selling-to-the-government-explaining-the-procurement-integrity-act.htm

[5] Former DOD officials lament shortcomings in relationship with contractors, June 03, 2016, Tony Bertuca

[6] Frank Kendall, Defense AT&L: November–December 2013

[7] From *Effective Vendor Engagement: Start the Conversation!* Joanie F. Newhart, CPCM, Associate Administrator for Acquisition Workforce Programs, Office of Federal Procurement Policy, Office of Management and Budget.

[8] Lauderdale III, *The Complete Idiots Guide to Getting Government Contracts*, 2009, Page 32

Chapter 21
Building
Relationships with
Govies

Garrison Keeler tells us that in the world of Lake Wobegon, "all the children are above average." In the real world of government contracts, we need to aim a little higher. At a minimum, we want to be in the 90th percentile when competing for customer relationships. And we certainly want to avoid the *Dunning-Kruger effect* where the least competent people in an area vastly overrate their skill levels.

Veterans of the contracting world are often asked by those new to the industry, "How do I get started? How do I meet people and begin to form a relationship?" Using the Relationship Continuum, they are asking, "How do I get to stage one? How do I get to the introduction and my first follow-up visits?"

Whether you're new to working with the government or a veteran, you need to sharpen your mindset of positive habits and smart activities to strengthen your customer relationship skills.

To launch yourself into the 90th percentile, there are two habits to practice. The first is the habit of shared experiences, and the second is the habit of bringing value.

Shared Experiences

There are two common forms of shared experience: professional and social. Both of these enable you to begin relationships that quietly move to the right on the Customer Relationship Continuum.

Let's look at why shared experiences matter:

"But one of the things that keeps face-to-face friendships strong is the nature of shared experience: you laugh together and you gape at the hot-dog eaters on Coney Island together. We do have a social-media equivalent – sharing, liking, and knowing that all of your friends have looked at the same cat video on YouTube as you did – but it lacks the synchronicity of shared experience. It's like a comedy that you watch by yourself: you won't laugh as loudly or as often, even if you're fully aware that all your friends think it's hysterical. We've seen the same movie, but we can't bond over it in the same way."[1]

"To really connect with others, you have to do more than find common ground and communicate well. You need to find a way to cement the relationship. Joseph F. Newton said, 'People are lonely because they build walls instead of bridges.' To build bridges that connects you to people in a lasting way, share common experiences with them. Share meals with people. Go to a ball game together. Take people out on a call or visitation with you. Anything you experience together that creates a common history helps to connect you to others."[2]

Following are some practical actions you can to take to meet customers and share experiences with them.

- Attend conferences and seminars.
    - o "Turn a casual conference attendance into a mission. Don't just be an attendee; be a conference commando!"[3]
    - o Execute *Rule 555* – Commit to a pre-targeted list of meeting 5 new customers, renewing 5 existing customers and making 5 introductions for coworkers.
- Attend dinners hosted by military branches.
- Meet customers at ceremonies such as change of command, award, and retirement ceremonies.
- Learn about associations that are pertinent to you.
    - o Note: "Publications, associations, and other pertinent Web sites are available at www.GovernmentMarketMaster.com.

One additional resource, Federal News Radio, is available at www.FederalNewsRadio.com."[4]

- Join professional associations and attend tradeshows such as:

  o AFCEA (Armed Forces Communications & Electronics Association)

  o Navy: Navy League, Naval Helicopter Association

  o Air Force: AFA (Air Force Association), Salute to ACC (Air Combat Command)

  o Army Aviation: AUSA (Association of the United States Army), AAAA (Army Aviation Association of America)

  o USMC: Marine Corps Association and Marine Corps Aviation Association

  o NCMA (National Contract Management Association)

If you join an association, I suggest that you actively participate. Don't sign up for a resume builder.

Social events are a great way to meet others and forge a relationship. A benefit of meeting people at social events apart from the work environment is that it removes ranks and puts people on a more equal footing. Consider:

- Attending golf or fishing outings.

- Playing in local base golf or softball leagues.

- Creating a mutual beneficial feeling. For example, sponsor or attend a golfing charity event for Wounded Warriors, USO, or the VA hospital. Mingle at an event that makes everyone feel good about themselves and their association.

- Help in a local community or charity drive event.

One important caution: When meeting socially with customers, be extremely careful about discussing business. Your goal is to build relationships, not blow them up. If the people you're with feel tricked or trapped because you keep talking business at what is supposed to be a social event, their guard will go up and their enjoyment down. And any desire for them to socialize with you in the future evaporates. Plan on a two-minute burst of business dialogue and go back to making the time with you pleasant, fun, and enjoyable. Any more, and you will be viewed as below average.

Another approach to build strong relationships is to collaborate when there is no ongoing procurement. For example:

- Co-author a joint paper on a topic about which you and a government employee are passionate.

- Serve together on a panel, task force, or board such as a DSB (Defense Science Board.)

- Co-brief at symposiums or tradeshows.

- Create a venue for building relationships such as hosting an event at a tradeshow. (By the way, it's legal as long as attendance is open to others, even your competitors.) Don't *sell* at the event; just build relationships and networks.

Bring Them Value

In the world of missiles, some missiles are equipped with a guidance system that, after launch, requires no further guidance. The missile can hit its target without the launcher being in line-of-sight with the target. This is called *fire and forget*. In building smart relationships, you can't just launch and leave. You need to consistently show up and bring value.

Customers value new, relevant, and timely information. Ways to bring value to your customers include:

- Information: Timely, relevant news on the program, a related news or trade journal article, language in the Congressional Record, etc.

- White papers: Substantive analysis on key issues and requirements, not self-serving product datasheets.

- Invitations to demonstrations or videos showing a demonstration: No marketing videos.

- Test data: Proving the existence theorem that the requirements are achievable at acceptable risk. This shows insight and the "art of the possible."

- Tradeoff matrix: Showing different ways to solve the problem versus the cost.

- Perspectives: Attitudes and perceptions of other government stakeholders.

- Early news: Especially any info that made his customers smart in front of their bosses.

- Connections: Connecting customers to the right person or authority on the topic.

If you want your customer to make time with you a priority, make it your priority to bring value to your customer.

While looking for ways to start relationships, don't ignore the importance of passing and receiving the relationship baton. The transfer of the relationship baton requires a concerted effort.

If you have a longtime relationship with a government employee, bring your colleagues/mentees to meet them and carry on the relationship. Resist the urge to be possessive of the relationship.

One senior industry executive had a stellar 25-year relationship with a DoD counterpart. They attended the weddings of their children and shared dinners regularly. This senior executive took his mentees to meet this Govie to carry on the relationship. Furthermore, they connected their respective direct reports for the next generation of relationships.

While staying in touch with your existing customers, be sure to stay in the habit of beginning new relationships. Keep developing your relationship growing skills; you are going to need them.

Dynamic changes are happening in the procurement world. As Mark Amtower stresses, the average age in the federal workforce is forty-seven and the average age at the SES (Senior Executive Service) is fifty-five, which makes these people eligible for retirement. Consequently, there will be significant exits of people from the workforce and a large influx of others joining it. This makes your relationship building skills more important than ever.

Start growing your relationship base now. As the saying goes, the best time to plant a tree is 20-years ago; the second best time is today. As Pugh and Bacon remind us, "Relationships don't spring to maturity overnight. It takes time to build a good relationship with anyone."[5]

Make sure you stay above average.

---

[1] http://www.newyorker.com/science/maria-konnikova/social-media-affect-math-dunbar-number-friendships

[2] Maxwell and Dornan, *How to Influence People*, 2013, Page 140-141

[3] Ferrazzi and Raz, *Never Eat Alone*, 2005, Page 110

[4] Amtower, *Selling to the Government*, 2011, Page 207

[5] Pugh and Bacon

Part Eight: Winning with Govies

Chapter 22
Fear: Your
Customer's Secret
Motivator

The acquisition process is ridiculously daunting. "The Lord's Prayer contains 56 words; the Gettysburg Address, 266 words; the Ten Commandments, 297 words; the preamble to the Declaration of Independence, 300 words. The U.S. Government specification describing a chocolate chip cookie contains 25,600 words!"[1]

Although the government can feel like a cold bureaucracy, it consists of people. People who have stressful daily lives, relentless pressures, and an aversion to risk. To serve them well, it helps to understand what the job of a Govie is like.

Respect Their Daily Lives

Government customers are often short on time, funding, and access to technical depth and experience. They run from meeting to meeting, respond to hundreds of emails a day, and have no time to be *sold* anything. And that's on a good day.

On a bad day, when a contractor's program is in trouble, they may have to dash off to the Pentagon to brief senior officials. Worse yet, on large programs, they may have to answer probing questions from the media, the GAO, or Congress.

On top of all this, they have more oversight, scrutiny, and bureaucracy than ever before. They have to deal with:

- An avalanche of changing regulations with countless provisions (Weapons Acquisition Reform Act of 2009, past National Defense Authorization Acts, Better Buying Power 1.0, 2.0, 3.0+, Acquisition Agility Act)

- Constant acquisition reform

- More independent cost estimation pressures

- More taxpayer watchdog organizations

- Increased media scrutiny

Ouch! And while attempting to keep up, they are fully aware that the world is becoming increasingly dangerous. It's difficult to achieve your most important mission outcomes when fighting resource shortages, distractions, and bureaucracy every day.

A Navy captain in charge of a 20-billion-dollar program was asked about her daily life. She responded, "I'm required to spend so much time explaining what I do to people scrutinizing this program that it interferes with my time to do what I'm supposed to do as the leader of this program."

Respect Their Pressure

Walk in the Govie's shoes, and you will quickly realize that they have a *buying problem*. They need to satisfy their radically diverse stakeholders and get through a challenging process – one filled with massive amounts of paperwork, bureaucracy, and arduous approvals. They don't want a high adventure roller coaster ride. They want a non-eventful program that stays on track and flies under the radar. The three primary goals of the PCO and the acquisition professional are to:

- Avoid anything that could jeopardize the integrity of the acquisition process.

- Avoid the appearance of impropriety based on unfair competitive advantage.

- Avoid any conflicts of interest or the appearance of conflicts.

While striving for these goals, there are other pressures and forces on a government buyer:

1. The end-user (their ultimate boss) wants and needs a better, faster, and cheaper solution.

2. The PCO represents the taxpayer and is focused on fostering competition, meeting the FAR, avoiding or withstanding a protest, and getting the lowest price.

3. Members of Congress care about gaining and maintaining jobs in their districts to get votes and increase their tax bases.

4. Senior officials care about not making a major acquisition mistake. They want a safe choice.

5. The SMEs want to be labeled as advanced technology gurus.

6. Everyone wants recognition and accolades for doing a great job on source selection. This recognition often supports cash awards later.

Within this milieu, Govies value contractors who understand their pressures and help them discover an approach that keeps everyone in the procurement system satisfied.

Respect Their Aversion to Risk

Within the contracting world, government acquisitions people are often remarkably unaware of the extraordinary expense, stress, and disruption that bidders endure as they attempt to submit proposals that are compliant and compelling.

Similarly, it's easy for bidders to forget what acquisitions teams experience as the award decision time approaches. They too can be nervous and lose sleep over the upcoming decision. They can be confused, frustrated, or skeptical of the claims made by bidders and fearful of the downstream consequences of a poor selection. And they worry about making a bad choice.

They wonder:

- Is the bidder going to *bait and switch* by showing me their A-Team to win and then deploying the C-Team to implement?

- Will I look like a smart decision maker if my selection is not the incumbent or a big-name company?

- Can I substantiate my decision with defensible facts and data?

- Do I risk a failed program or lose credibility if I choose this bidder?

In these critical moments, acquisition officials can easily get entangled in a cognitive battle known as *approach/avoidance*. It is a psychological dance where the negative emotion of fear pulls rank over the positive desire for the best solution.

As the time to select the *best choice* contractor approaches, the desire to avoid a *poor choice* increases. When this occurs, the safety of a known, trusted relationship with a bidder can hold significant sway in the final award decision. This compelling desire for a safe choice with the least risk is perfectly understandable. It's human nature for individuals to protect their own self-interests.

"If you press people to identify the motives behind their self-interest it usually boils down to four items: money, power, status and popularity."[2]

Amazingly, all four items listed above – money, power, status, and popularity – are in play when award decisions are made.

"Federal government procurement, after all, is people – contract officers, technical staffs, agency executives, auditors, inspectors, contract administrators – the buyocrats. A common fear pervades all bureaucracy, the black mark on a personnel record. That alone can disturb an otherwise normal progression up the government career ladder. The government has none of the conventional benchmark goals of the commercial marketplace – no sales quotas, no profit targets, no productivity ratings. The buyocrat's real stimulus is a negative factor; avoiding a bad proficiency report. And nothing creates a career black mark like a problem contract. No wonder that project offices are leery of bids that could be won by inexperienced prols or unknown firms; they could jeopardize a long career record. A sole source given to a trusted privileged or prime firm is the buyocrat's security blanket."[3]

To understand this better-safe-than-sorry perspective, we need to understand the buyer's fear of loss.

"In 2010, researchers at the University of Toronto wrote a paper about an experiment in a factory where workers were told one of two things about a weekly bonus. One group was told they would receive the bonus if they reached certain production targets. The other group was told they were provisionally awarded the bonus – it was theirs, but it would be taken away if they didn't reach their production targets.

"Even though the targets were the same, the group that was provisionally awarded the bonus outperformed the other group. Also to make sure the results weren't a fluke, the researchers continued the test over time, with consistent results. **Researchers concluded that the fear of loss was a greater motivator than the desire of a potential gain**."[4]

This effect has even been quantified. "Desire for gain has a motivational power of 1.0. But fear of loss has a negative motivational power of 2.5. In other words, the fear of loss is two and a half times more powerful than the desire for gain. People are much more motivated to buy if they feel they are going to lose something by not buying, than they are in anticipation of the benefits they will enjoy if they do buy."[5]

Govies are no different. They are more motivated by fear than the upside of success. Govies ask, "Who are these people? Can I trust them? Should I risk the reputation that I've built for 20-years? What are the worst things that could happen?"

There are five *nevers* that customers _never_ want to happen to them or their teams:

1. *Never miss the IOC (Initial Operational Capability)*

2. *Never miss a delivery in the fielding plan*

3. *Never experience these nightmare outcomes:*

   a. *Show cause letter, termination, GAO investigation, rampant cost or schedule growth*

   b. *Nunn-McCurdy breach or Congressional budget zeroing for failure to comply with their language*

4. *Never go back to the well a second time for more money or time*

5. *Never fail late in testing*

[Note: For ACAT-1 programs, a Nunn-McCurdy breach could occur when the cost overrun exceeds 25%. (According to the Congressional

Research Service, from 2007 to 2013, there were 22 critical breaches and 12 significant breaches.) Terminations for convenience or default are fairly unlikely. But cost growth, late deliveries and less than promised operational performance is all too likely.]

While seeking to solve your customers' greatest challenges, remain mindful of their stressful daily lives, relentless pressures, and aversion to risk. Understand that government customers are seeking help, assurance, and a safe choice. Make it part of your mission to move them from a state of fear and mistrust to one of confidence and assurance.

There is one last fear Govies live with. It is the honorable fear of failing the warfighters. That single fear should warrant your deepest respect and your finest efforts.

---

[1] Amtower, *Selling to the Government*, 2011, Page 19

[2] Goldsmith, *What Got You Here Won't Get You There*, 2007, Page 30

[3] Robertson, *Selling to the Federal Government*, 1979, Pages 32-33

[4] Schultz and Doerr, *Insight Selling*, 2014, Page 89

[5] Tracy, *The Psychology of Selling, 2004,* Page 58

Chapter 23
The Power of the
Personal Win Wish

The only way on earth to influence other people is to talk about what they want and show them how to get it.[1]

Contractors spend countless hours and small fortunes studying customer RFPs. Their goal is to be fully compliant while demonstrating their understanding of the customer's needs and their ability to meet or exceed them. All of this is necessary. But it's easy to get so absorbed in the line-by-line analysis of the RFP that they lose sight of the big picture and forget that customers have their own personal wish lists. They have self-interests that matter greatly to them.

The art and craft of selling is understanding the connection between your proposal and *their* self-interest. Part of their self-interest is to learn what it would be like to work with you.

"You always undergo a chemistry test with customers. Once they have decided that you're competent – that you can do the job – the critical question in their decision making is not, 'Who can do the work?' Rather it is, 'With whom do we want to work?'"[2]

"How will it be to work with this supplier? Even if they can deliver, *can we work with them*? Do they have *both the capability and the chemistry* we're seeking?"[3]

The customer hopes to avoid being sold the dream and living the nightmare. They don't want PowerPoint heaven to turn into program hell. They fear selecting providers who promise more than they can deliver. They want to avoid those who give them headaches and panic attacks. They want someone who will make their lives a little easier while making their programs successful.

That's why the contractor who has deep trust with the customer has a huge competitive advantage. They not only have the greatest probability of understanding the *overt* requirements of the RFP, they also have the best understanding of the *covert* requirements that are never stated. They know what's on the customer's wish list.

"Buyers make emotional decisions based on what they want to achieve and what they want to avoid – gains and pains. Personal gains include things people want more of: control, image, power, security, stability, ego gratification, and greed, to name just a few. Fears include what they want less of: risk, more work to do, too much exposure, a call at 2:00 A.M. asking where the supplies are, loss of control, damage to their image, political vulnerability, making a mistake, and other pain areas."[4]

To grasp your customer's personal priorities, note what Mark Goulston writes in *Just Listen*: "Does the customer feel felt? Do you take the customer to the 'ICU'? The ICU is what are Important, Critical, and Urgent to the customer (not to you.)"[5]

Want to know what is vital to your customers? They want you to grasp that they are putting their careers on your shoulders and *that* is important, critical, and urgent to them. Their secret wish is: "Don't screw this up. Don't embarrass me. Don't drag me though a protest or program failure."

The GO Matrix: A Safe Choice and a Personal Win

Source selection customers are trying to ascertain which bidder provides them a safe choice and a personal win. They are asking themselves: *Will my agency and I both be better off in the future with this bidder?*

The 2x2 GO (Government Outcome) Matrix below represents the desire of source selection customers to move from fear to safe, and from failure to a personal win.

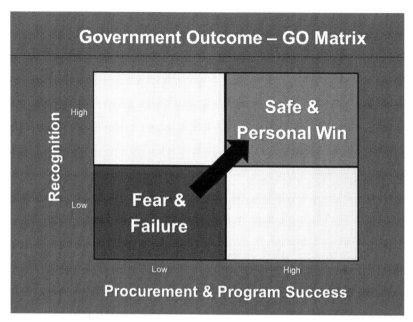

From the customer's perspective, they feel safe working with brands and people they trust. To them, the safe choice is the smart choice.

Your task is to legitimately move customers to the upper-right quadrant where they feel safe and likely to experience a personal win if they select you. Rethink what they want and re-evaluate what you give. Make granting personal wins a subtle benefit feature of your offering. Make it your priority to make your customer successful in the eyes of their stakeholders.

Look up from the line-by-line analysis of the RFP, and you will re-discover the unique world of acquisitions officials working in government.

Unlike business-to-business selling, Govies are not motivated by profit. They are motivated by service to their country. They are often patriotic and committed to providing the best products for the front lines to defend our country.

Paralleling these desires are their personal wish list of things that are legitimately important to them. These criteria are not verbally stated and you will not read them in the RFP. But they can, at times, trump the stated RFP criteria and be a major factor in determining who wins or loses the award. They are worth knowing and respecting. I call them:

The Acquisition Official's Wish List:
The Ten Attributes of a Personal Win

The Procurement Wish

1. A bulletproof, defensible, fair selection decision that is awarded without a protest.

2. If a procurement is protested, the process and decision withstands the scrutiny of an agency or GAO protest.

3. A procurement that is so successful it becomes a best-practice case study and the acquisition officials receive recognition or awards.

The Program Wish

4. A no-failure program. (An unsuccessful program can be a devastating loss for the customer. It can be career limiting for individuals and negatively impact an agency's reputation.)

5. A highly successful program. (A successful program is a personal win for a Govie program manager. It can result in increased responsibility, the opportunity to manage an ACAT-1 (Acquisition Category 1) program, or the chance to be promoted to a PEO (Program Executive Officer) who manages multiple programs.)

6. Selecting a bidder who executes. (A personal win is the selection of the bidder that successfully delivers mission value to the end-user within reasonable constraints of cost and schedule.)

7. Smooth is good. (Customers prefer a well-run program to a white-knuckle, scary roller coaster program.)

The Legacy Wish

8. A successful acquisition and program implementation that provides a fast lane to promotion.

9. A positive legacy. (Many acquisition officials desire to leave their mark on a successful program before they leave their post or retire.)

10. A legacy launch pad. (A positive legacy enables retiring military to launch a second career as consultants, lobbyists, or to take business development positions within industry.)

If you are new to the acquisition world, there are several other facts and factors worth knowing.

- It can be a personal win for an OSD (Office of Secretary of Defense) lead if two or more services align to form a joint program where commonality saved taxpayer money.

- It can be a personal win for the Competition Advocate or Department of Justice anti-trust lawyers to bust up a potential monopoly.

- On occasion, different services jockey to take the lead on a joint program or they try to get rid of another service to avoid a joint program. Still yet, they may compete with another service to get the lead in a mission area. (The DoD Services are all on the same team in theatre when they fight shoulder-to-shoulder, but in DC politics, there are often rivalries. These service sibling-like competitions are real, and it's worthwhile to be aware of their possible presence and power.)

- Typically, there is a *one-year cooling-off period* when those in the acquisition community are prohibited from working in their same industry. This is to avoid Organizational Conflict of Interest (OCI).

- It's helpful to understand the GS (General Schedule) Scale to understand the positions of people working in government. Within the government, positions range from a GS-1 to GS-15. The GS-9 is considered comparable to a first lieutenant (O-2), while a GS-15, the top of the General Schedule, is the equivalent grade of a colonel or captain.

- Within the Senior Executive Service (SES) positions range from SES-1 to SES-6. Senior Executive Service and Senior Level grades correspond for protocol purposes to flag and general officers (admirals and generals).

Summary

Remember that customers in the acquisition community take great pride in their work. You will serve them and yourself well when you honor their pride, respect their concerns, and grant them their personal wishes.

It also helps to remember that, like you and me, they are human.

"Like most people, federal managers hate being wrong since it affects their career file. For the most part, they just want to do a good job, avoid problems and go home to their kids' soccer games. So don't create headaches for them."[6]

When you look up from the RFP, be sure to rediscover the values that matter and the signals you want to send:

"Embrace values that should have always mattered in the first place. Honesty. Transparency. Empathy. These traits build long-term relationships. Traits that send out signals that people can trust you, and that it's safe to do business with you. But more important, traits that define us as human beings."[7]

Make your customers feel safe and grant them their personal wish. They will sleep better at night and thank you by day.

Mindset Tips:

✓ Customers are afraid of "Being sold the dream and living the nightmare." To grant wins, remove their fears and de-risk their goals. Make your customer a hero.

✓ Empathize with the customer's negative inner thoughts:

- o Don't screw this up.

- o Don't embarrass me.

- o Don't drag me through the pain of a protest or bad performance.

---

[1] McGee, *How to Succeed With People*, 2013, Page 144
[2] Pugh and Bacon, *Powerful Proposals*, 2005, Page 13
[3] Pugh and Bacon, *Powerful Proposals*, 2005, Page 58
[4] Reilly, *Value Added Selling*, 2010, Page 85
[5] Mark Goulston, *Just Listen* (AMACOM, 2010)
[6] White, *Rolling the Dice in DC*, 2006, Page 78-78
[7] Michael Maslansky & Scott West, *"The Language of Trust"* Penguin Group, 2010-03-10

Wrap-up

The former Deputy Secretary of Defense, David Packard, is known for his incisive comment: "We all know what needs to be done. The question is, 'Why aren't we doing it?'" When it comes to customer relationships, it's now your turn to know what needs to be done, and then do it.

It Is Time to Remember

- Remember "The E of L = R." (The essence of life equals relationships.)

- Remember, organizations that win, grow, and keep government business differentiate themselves from their competition by doing three things well. First, they fully embrace customer relationships as a *Mission Set*. Second, they relentlessly cultivate a *Mindset* of customer focus throughout their entire organization. On a daily basis the customer-focused mindset is taught, discussed, modeled, celebrated, and expected. And third, they invest in teaching every employee the *Skill Sets* necessary to cultivate smart customer relationships.

- Remember, the "X" Factor of smart customer relationships has a rational explanation with progressive dividends:

Those who learn the skill of developing a smart relationship with the customer are most likely to have greater ease of access to the customer.

Ease of access to the customer enables you to have more valuable time with the customer.

More time with your customer enables you to have greater understanding of your customer.

More understanding of your customer gives you legal intelligence into the customer's needs, pressures, pain points, and priorities.

Deeper intelligence about your customer enables you to more effectively bring specific value and iterate problem-solving solutions to your customer.

Your intelligence, specific value, and problem-solving solutions can then be represented in a "custom fit" proposal to the customer that clearly differentiates you from the competition.

It Is Time to Decide

- Decide to intentionally push your relationship with your customer to the right on the Relationship Continuum.

- Decide to qualitatively evaluate where you are on the Relationship Continuum with your customer.

- Decide to keep the ten relationship winning mindsets at the forefront of your mind in each customer encounter. Before every customer interaction, review the list below and then select several to implement.

The 10 Relationship Winning MINDSETS

- *MINDSET #1:* The Power of Microbursts

  Look for microbursts of genuine human moments with your customer and the meta-messages from your customer.

- *MINDSET #2:* The Power of Caring

  Remember, people don't care how much you know until they know how much you care. Impress them with your genuineness, not your genius.

- *MINDSET #3:* The Power of Awareness

  Practice your skills of Situational Awareness, Self-awareness, and Other People Awareness. (Remember to SNL: shut up, notice, and listen!)

- *MINDSET #4:* The Power of Smart Listening

  Turn on your sensors and learn to listen so well that you can hear what is undetectable to others.

- *MINDSET #5:* The Power of Smart Silence

  Make it your habit to keep the spotlight of time and attention on your customer and not on you and your company. Don't be a "Me Monster."

- *MINDSET #6:* The Power of Smart Questions

  Decide to practice the skill of asking brilliant questions rather than trying to be the person with brilliant answers.

- *MINDSET #7:* The Power of Smart Trust

  Your customer is looking for someone whose competence, commitment, and character can be trusted. Decide to be that person. No matter what.

- *MINDSET #8:* The Power of Smart Networking

  Make it your priority to grow a network of people whom you can serve. Practice the joy of being the one who serves others and give up the urge to be the one served by others.

- *MINDSET #9:* The Power of Smart Emotion

  Be mindful that reducing real or perceived risks is a primary concern of your customer. Fear is a secret driver in their decision process. Help them manage it.

- *MINDSET #10:* The Power of the Personal Win Wish

  Make your customer a hero in their world. Serve them and set them up for extraordinary success.

I welcome you to make one other decision. Decide to stay in touch. Feel free to share your thoughts, comments and questions with me. It would be my pleasure to hear from you.

Contact me at Tom@CommunicationGuys.com

Order information for *Billion Dollar Mindsets* at www.CommunicationGuys.com

Bibliography

1. David D. Acker, *Skill in Communication* (Defense Systems Management College, 1992.)
2. Mark Amtower, *Selling to the Government* (Hoboken, NJ: John Wiley & Sons, Inc., 2011.)
3. Paul Arden, *It's Not How Good You Are, It's How Good You Want To Be* (New York: Phaidon Press, 2003.)
4. Terry R. Bacon, Ph.D., *Creating Preference*, (APMP; Association of Proposal Management Professionals, Fall/Winter, 2002.)
5. Terry R. Bacon, Ph.D., *Selling to Major Accounts* (New York: AMACOM, 1999.)
6. Terry R. Bacon & David G. Pugh, *Winning Behavior* (New York: AMACOM, 2003.)
7. Jeb Blount, *Fanatical Prospecting* (Hoboken, NJ: John Wiley & Sons, Inc., 2015.)
8. Jeb Blount, *People Buy You* (Hoboken, NJ: John Wiley & Sons, Inc., 2010.)
9. Travis Bradberry & Jean Greaves, *Emotional Intelligence 2.0* (San Diego: TalentSmart, 2009.)
10. Bob Burg and John David Mann, *Go-Givers Sell More* (New York: Portfolio/Penguin, 2010.)
11. Dale Carnegie, *How to Win Friends & Influence People* (New York: Pocket Books, 1936.)
12. Robert B. Cialdini, *Harnessing the Science of Persuasion* (Article from HBR OnPoint, Harvard Business School Publishing, 2001.)
13. Stephen M.R. Covey, *The Speed of Trust* (New York: Free Press, 2006.)
14. Stephen M.R. Covey and Greg Link, *Smart Trust* (New York: Free Press, 2012.)
15. Chris Denove and James D. Power IV, *Satisfaction* (New York: Portfolio/Penguin, 2007.)
16. Matthew Dixon and Brent Adamson, *The Challenger Sale* (New York: Portfolio/Penguin, 2011.)
17. Nancy Duarte, *Resonate* (Hoboken: John Wiley & Sons, Inc., 2010.)
18. Fredrik Eklund, *The Sell* (New York: Penguin Random House, 2015.)
19. Keith Ferrazzi with Tahl Raz, *Never Eat Alone* (Currency/Doubleday, 2005.)

20. Jeffrey J. Fox, *How to Become a Rainmaker* (New York: Hyperion, 2000.)
21. Richard C. Freed, Shervin Freed and Joe Romano, *Writing Winning Business Proposals: Your Guide to Landing the Client, Making the Sale and Persuading the Boss* (McGraw-Hill, 1995.)
22. Don Gabor, *How to Start a Conversation and Make Friends* (New York: Fireside, 2001.)
23. Carmine Gallo, *Talk Like Ted (*New York: St. Martin's Press, 2014.)
24. Jeffrey Gitomer, *Little Black Book of Connections* (Austin: Bard Press, 2006.)
25. Garber, Peter. "101 Ways to Build Customer Relationships." Demo, 2007. iBooks.
26. Seth Godin, *All Marketers Are Liars* (New York: Portfolio/Penguin, 2012.)
27. Marshall Goldsmith with Mark Reiter, *What Got You Here Won't Get You There* (New York: Hachette Books, 2007.)
28. Mark Goulston, *Just Listen* (AMACOM, 2010.)
29. Claire M. Grady, Director, Defense Procurement and Acquisition Policy, *DoD Source Selection Procedures*, 4/1/2016.
30. Adam Grant, *Give and Take* (New York: Penguin Books, 2013.)
31. Robert M. Hansen, *Winning Strategies for Capturing Defense Contracts* (Arlington, VA: Gloria Magnus Publishing, 1992.)
32. Andy Harrington, *Passion into Profit* (United Kingdom: John Wiley & Sons Ltd, 2015.)
33. Harvard Business Review, *On Emotional Intelligence* (Boston: Harvard Business Review Press, 2015.)
34. Ron Hoff, *Say It in Six* (Barnes & Noble, Inc., 1996.)
35. Chet Holmes, *The Ultimate Sales Machine* (New York: Penguin Group, 2007.)
36. Tony Jeary, *Leverage* (Franklin, Tennessee: Clovercroft Publishing, 2014.)
37. Frances Cole Jones, *How to Wow* (New York: Ballantine Books, 2009.)
38. Marshall H. Kaplan, *Acquiring Major Systems Contracts* (New York: John Wiley & Sons, Inc., 1988.)
39. Guy Kawasaki, *Enchantment* (New York: Portfolio/Penguin, 2011.)
40. Scott Keyser, *Winner Takes All – Seven-and-a-half principles for winning more bids, tenders, and proposals* (London: LID Publishing Ltd, London, 2014.)
41. Mahan Khalsa and Randy Illig, Let's Get Real or Let's Not Play (New York: Penguin Group, 2008.)
42. Oren Klaff, *Pitch Anything*, (McGraw-Hill, 2011.)

43. John C. Lauderdale III, *The Complete Idiot's Guide to Getting Government Contracts* (New York: Penguin Group, 2009.)
44. Bob Lohfeld, *How and when to talk to your customer, Bob Lohfeld tracks the misconceptions about communications during the procurement process* (June 18, 2014.)
45. Lohfeld Consulting Group, Inc., Edited by Beth Wingate, *Best Informed Wins, Collected Articles of Bob Lohfeld from Washington Technology (USA: Lohfeld Consulting Group, Inc.*, 2010-2012.)
46. Lohfeld Consulting Group, Inc., Edited by Beth Wingate, *Best Informed Wins, Volume 2, Collected Articles of Bob Lohfeld from Washington Technology (USA: Lohfeld Consulting Group, Inc.*, 2013-2015.)
47. Lohfeld Consulting Group, Inc., Edited by Beth Wingate, *Insights, Capture & Proposal Insights & Tips* (Maryland: Lohfeld Consulting Group, Inc., 2012.)
48. Jack Malcolm, *Bottom-Line Selling* (Seattle: Booktrope Editions, 2011.)
49. Jack Malcolm, *Strategic Sales Presentations* (Seattle: Booktrope Editions, 2010.)
50. Michael Maslansky and Scott West. *The Language of Trust*, Penguin Group, 2010.
51. John C. Maxwell, *Relationships 101, What Every Leader Needs to Know* (Nashville: Thomas Nelson, 2003.)
52. John C. Maxwell, *Winning with People, Discover the People Principles that Work for You Every Time* (Nashville: Thomas Nelson, 2008.)
53. John C. Maxwell and Jim Dornan, *How to Influence People* (Nashville: Thomas Nelson, 2013.)
54. Paul McGee, *How to Succeed With People* (United Kingdom: Capstone Publishing Ltd, 2013.)
55. Robert B. Miller and Stephen E. Heiman, *Conceptual Selling* (Miller-Heiman, Inc. Walnut Creek, CA, 1987.)
56. Robert B. Miller and Stephen E. Heiman with Tad Tuleja, *The New Successful Large Account Management* (New York: Time Warner Book Group, 2005.)
57. Terri Morrison and Wayne A. Conaway, *Kiss, Bow, or Shake Hands* (Avon, MA: Adams Media, 2006.)
58. Alex Osterwalder, Yves Pigneur, Greg Bernarda and Alan Smith, *Value Proposition Design* (Hoboken: John Wiley & Sons, Inc., 2014.)
59. Erik Peterson and Tim Riesterer, *Conversations That Win The Complex Sale* (New York: McGraw-Hill, 2011.)
60. Daniel H. Pink, *To Sell is Human* (New York: Riverhead Books, 2012.)
61. David G. Pugh and Terry R. Bacon, *Powerful Proposals* (New York: AMACOM, 2005.)

62. David G. Pugh, Ph.D., *Proposing To Win, Fifth Edition* (Durango, CO: Lore International Institute, 2005.)

63. Fred Reichheld, *The Ultimate Question* (Boston: Harvard Business School Press, 2006.)

64. Fred Reichheld with Rob Markey, *The Ultimate Question 2.0* (Boston: Bain & Company, 2011.)

65. Tom Reilly, *Value-Added Selling* (New York: McGraw Hill, 2010.)

66. Jack W. Robertson, *Selling to the Federal Government* (New York: McGraw-Hill, Inc., 1979.)

67. Mark Rodgers, *Persuasion Equation* (AMACOM, 2015.)

68. Robert Schieffer, *Ten Key Customer Insights* (Thomson, 2005.)

69. Mike Schultz and John E. Doerr, *Insight Selling* (Hoboken, NJ: John Wiley & Sons, Inc., 2014.)

70. G. Richard Shell and Mario Moussa, *the art of Woo* (New York: Penguin Group, 2007.)

71. Jagdish Sheth and Andrew Sobel, *Clients for Life* (New York: Simon & Schuster, 2000.)

72. Shipley Associates, *Shipley Capture Guide, Winning Strategic Business* (Farmington, UT: Shipley Associates, 2008.)

73. Felicia J. Slattery, *Kill the Elevator Speech* (Shippensburg, PA: Sound Wisdom, 2014.)

74. Paul Smith, *Lead with A Story* (AMACOM, 2012.)

75. Olessia Smotrova-Taylor, *How to Get Government Contracts* (New York: Apress, 2012.)

76. Andrew Sobel, *All for One* (Hoboken, NJ: John Wiley & Sons, Inc., 2009.)

77. Andrew Sobel, *Making Rain* (Hoboken, NJ: John Wiley & Sons, Inc., 2003.)

78. Andrew Sobel & Jerold Panas, *Power Questions* (Hoboken, NJ: John Wiley & Sons, Inc., 2012.)

79. Andrew Sobel and Jerold Panas, *Power Relationships, 26 Irrefutable Laws for Building Extraordinary Relationships* (Hoboken: John Wiley & Sons, Inc., 2014.)

80. Success Magazine, October 2015.

81. Corey Summers and David Jenkins, *Whiteboard Selling, Empowering Sales through visuals* (Hoboken, NJ: John Wiley & Sons, Inc.)

82. *Stanford Encyclopedia of Philosophy, Aristotle's Rhetoric* http://plato.stanford.edu/entries/aristotle-rhetoric/#mean_(First published Thu May 2, 2002.)

83. George J. Thompson, Ph.D., and Jerry B. Jenkins, *Verbal Judo* (Harper Collins, 2004.)

84. Jeff Thull, *Mastering the Complex Sale – How to Compete and Win when the Stakes are High!* (Hoboken, NJ: John Wiley & Sons, Inc., 2003.)

85. Brian Tracy, *The Psychology of Selling* (Nashville: Thomas Nelson, 2004.)
86. Dave Ulrich & Norm Smallwood, *Why the Bottom Line Isn't!* (Hoboken: John Wiley & Sons, Inc., 2003.)
87. William Ury, *Getting to Yes with Yourself and Other Worthy Opponents* (New York: HarperCollins, 2015.)
88. Gary Walker, *The Customer Centric Selling Field Guide to Prospecting and Business Development* (New York: McGraw Hill, 2013.)
89. Richard White, *Rolling the Dice in DC* (Richard J. White, Wood River Technologies, Inc. and Fedmarket.com, 2006.)
90. Jerry R. Wilson, *151 Quick Ideas to Get New Customers* (Pompton Plains, NJ: Career Press, 2005.)
91. Zig Ziglar, *Secrets of Closing the Sale* (New York: Berkley Books, 1984.)

Resources

- http://www.acqnotes.com/
- Glossary of Acquisition Terms (Federal Acquisition Institute): www.fai.gov/pdfs/glossary.pdf
- "Publications, associations, and other pertinent Web sites are available at www.GovernmentMarketMaster.com. One additional resource, Federal News Radio, is available at www.FederalNewsRadio.com." [Amtower, Selling to the Government, 2011, Page 207].
- Myth-Busting memorandum, Addressing the Misconceptions to Improve Communication with Industry During the Acquisition Process
- Myth-Busting–2 memorandum, Addressing the Misconceptions and Further Improving Communication with Industry During the Acquisition Process

Acronyms

AAAA	Army Aviation Association of America
AFA	Air Force Association
AFCEA	Armed Forces Communications & Electronics Association
ACAT	Acquisition Category
ACC	Air Combat Command
AoA	Analysis of Alternatives
AT&L	Acquisition, Technology and Logistics
AUSA	Association of the United States Army
APB	Acquisition Program Baseline
APMP	Association of Proposal Management Professionals
ASP	Acquisition Strategy Panel
BAA	Broad Area Announcement
BCS	Best-case scenario
BD	Business Development
B&P	Bid and Proposal funds
BLUF	Bottom Line Up Front
BPP	Better Buying Power
CDD	Capability Development Document
CO	Contracting Officer
COI	Conflict of Interest
COTR	Contracting Officer's Technical Representatives
CPAR	Contractor Performance Assessment Report
CRM	Customer Relationship Management
CRP	Customer Relationship Plan
DAU	Defense Acquisition University

DARPA	Defense Advanced Research Projects Agency
DCAA	Defense Contract Audit Agency
DFAR	Defense Federal Acquisition Regulation
DISC®	Dominance, Influence, Steadiness, Conscientious
DoD	Department of Defense
DRFP	Draft Request for Proposal
DSB	Defense Science Board
E of L =R	The Essence of Life Equals Relationships
ECS	Emotional Competent Stimulus
E.E.I.	Essential Elements of Information
EN	Evaluation Notice
EN1	Emotional Needs First
EQ	Emotion Quotient
F2F	Face to face
FAR	Federal Acquisition Regulation
F.I.T.	Final Intimacy Test
fMRI	functional Magnetic Resonance Imaging
FMS	Foreign Military Sales
FPR	Final Proposal Revision
FRS	False Relationship Syndrome
FWA	Fraud, Waste or Abuse
FUD	Fear, Uncertainty and Doubt
GAO	Government Accountability Office
GO	Government Outcome
Govies	Nickname for Government employees
GS	The GS (general schedule) is separated into 15 grades (GS-1, GS-2, etc. up to GS-15)
ICU	Important, Critical, and Urgent to the customer
IFF	Identify Friend or Foe
IOC	Initial Operational Capability
IR&D	Internal Research and Development
LPTA	Lowest Priced Technically Acceptable

MBTI®	Myers-Briggs Type Indicator
MDA	Milestone Decision Authority
MIRs	Most Important Requirements
M-M-F-I	Make Me Feel important
NCMA	National Contract Management Association
NDA	Non-Disclosure Agreement
NDAA	National Defense Authorization Act
NMAM	National Military Appreciation Month
NMW	No Meeting Wednesday
NSA	National Security Agency
OCI	Organizational Conflict of Interest
OFPP	Office of Federal Procurement Policy
OMB	Office of Management and Budget
OODA	Observe, Orient, Decide, and Act
OPC	Other Person Centric
OPI	Other People's Interest
OSD	Office of the Secretary of Defense
PCO	Procuring Contracting Officer
PEO	Program Executive Officer
PI	Principle Investigator
PIC	Procurement Improvement Committee
PM	Program Manager
PTT	Push-to-Talk
Pwin	Probability of Win
RFI	Request for Information
RFP	Request for Proposal
RFP #'s	• RFP #1 is the Request for Proposal. • RFP #2 is the customer's Real Felt Pain. • RFP #3 is Really Fabulous People. • RFP #4 is Really Fabulous Presentation.
RO	Requirements Owner
ROI	Return of Invest

RMS	Reliability, Maintainability, and Supportability
RTW	Relationships That Win
S.A.D.S.	Self-Awareness Deficiency Syndrome
SBIR	Small Business Innovation Research
Section M	Evaluation Criteria in a Government RFP
SDR	System Design Review
SES	Senior Executive Service
SETA	Systems Engineering and Technical Assistance
SLO	Single Listening Objective
SME	Subject Matter Expert
SNL	Shut-up, Notice, Listen
SOO	Statement of Objectives
SOW	Statement of Work
S.P.I.C.E.	Sincerity, Passion, Interest, Curiosity, and Enthusiasm
SSA	Source Selection Authority
SSAC	Source Selection Advisory Council
SSEB	Source Selection Evaluation Board
SSP	Source Selection Plan
SST	Source Selection Team
SUIT-R	See, Understand, Improve The Relationships
T&Cs	Terms and Conditions
TIFOC	Time In Front of the Customer
TOE	Turn Off Electronics
T.O.P.	Time of Possession
USG	United States Government
VATEP	Value Adjusted Total Evaluated Price
WAIT	Why Am I Talking?
WIIFM	What's In It For Me?

About the Author

Dr. Tom Barrett is cofounder of the Communication Guys and Tightrope Communications. Tom specializes in teaching customer relationships, emotional intelligence, and communication skills.

Within the defense/government contracting industry he has trained thousands of people and has been instrumental in contractors winning in excess of $30 billion in new business.

Dr. Barrett is a frequent speaker at corporate conventions and has spoken at the United Nations, CIA, NASA, and the Pentagon. He is known for bringing an extraordinary blend of humor, business insights, and psychological wisdom to his keynote speeches and training workshops.

On Capitol Hill, he leads a weekly bi-partisan leadership class for Members of Congress. Tom has spent over 10,000 hours meeting one-on-one with Members of the Senate and the House of Representatives. He is one of the few individuals ever asked to address the orientation for new Members of Congress in *both* political parties.

He graduated summa cum laude while pursuing two master's degrees and a Ph.D. in psychology. Tom is the author of four other books, two of which are national best sellers with sales exceeding one million copies.

Tom is an avid golfer, skier, and outdoorsman. He and his wife, Linda, reside in Leesburg, VA.

To Order Copies of *Billion Dollar Mindsets*

Go to CommunicationGuys.com/BillionDollarMindsets

For bulk orders please contact us directly on
tom@CommunicationGuys.com

For Training and Speaking Engagements

Please send inquiries to tom@CommunicationGuys.com

Made in the USA
Middletown, DE
03 June 2017